WRITING FOR WELLNESS

Surviving Lockdown One Word at a Time

OLIVIA MCCABE

DEDICATION

For the members of Writing for Wellness, Shenley

CONTENTS

ACKNOWLEDGMENTS

I am full of gratitude to everyone who has ever uttered a kind or encouraging word about my work but there are a few that I would like to acknowledge as being instrumental in helping me get this book to print. I would like to thank God for being the source of my inspiration, and indeed the very air that I breathe, both in and out. A huge thank you to my family, both near and far, for all their love over the years, and for instilling in me, through both nature and nurture, a love of reading and writing. A special thanks to my mum for all her practical support during the writing of this book. Thanks to Lesley for her undying enthusiasm and encouragement, and J for hers. Thanks also to Ros for telling me to just write a blooming book regardless. Thanks to the other members of the Writing for Wellness group for their willingness and trust in me, for the other writers in the #writingcommunity on Twitter who are always so supportive, and finally, but by no means least, a huge thank you to my cat, Henry, for good cuddles at the end of long days. I couldn't have done it without any of you and am eternally grateful.

INTRODUCTION

Congratulations on taking the plunge and buying this book! In the Spring of 2020, at the height of the COVID-19 pandemic, I began a Writing for Wellness community here in Hertfordshire, England. Over the weeks, as we have met online, the community has grown, both in number and in self-awareness. There is such a strong sense of love, safety and support in the room. We have journeyed together through the highs and the lows, sharing our hopes, dreams, joys and fears with one another as we have gone along.

This book reflects that journey. It is my hope, that no matter where you are in the world, you will be inspired to write your way to Wellness and survive lockdown one word at a time. Perhaps, you may even be inspired to start your own Writing for Wellness group. Each chapter looks at different ways to engage in the Writing for Wellness process. From Inspiration to Imagination, from Humour to our Darkest Sides, the stories and activities within these pages guide us on a journey both within and without.

Having a background in publishing and public relations, I have always been fascinated by the craft of writing. Working in ministry, I have also explored the connection between writing, health and spirituality. As a writer and blogger of over twenty years, it has been a privilege for me to engage with many other writers around the world, and to delve deep into the question of what inspires us, where imagination comes from, and how writing it out leads to a fuller, more joyful existence.

As one lady said, "this group is the highlight of my week." It is my hope, that during lockdown and beyond, this book will be the highlight of your week too. What are you waiting for? Dive on in. And remember to share your experiences online using the hashtag #writingforwellness. Let's begin!

1 IMAGINATION

Alice Walker once said, "If you fall in love with the imagination, you understand that it is a free spirit. It will go anywhere, and it can do anything." During this time of lockdown, when global travel is severely restricted, and many of us cannot even leave our own homes, the imagination is perhaps more important to us than it has ever been before.

I don't know about you, but I love watching interviews with children when they're asked to describe something. They use words that have yet to be dreamed of and conjure up things into being that have yet to exist. My own nephew is a case in point. He wrote a whole book in which he drew and described new creatures with the most hilarious of names and the most bizarre of bodies.

Children can be entertaining and charming, but of course we adults have responsibilities, don't we? We can't indulge ourselves in fantasy as children can. We talked about this in the group. Members said that they felt they didn't have an imagination. They lacked confidence to simply write what they felt or what they dreamed about. They were shy about expressing themselves with words.

But the imagination is as vital an ingredient in life as is reason or intuition. Without it we cannot begin to conceive of a different and better world. Without imagination, everything stays the same, and in a world where we are surrounded by a global pandemic, surely, we want to dream of the life beyond lockdown? Let's begin our journey with a little experiment.

Activity One: When is a House a Home?

Take a piece of paper and fold it into eight sections. In section one, draw a house. Don't spend too long thinking about it. Just draw the first thing that comes into your head. Have you done it? Move on to the next task.

In the next section, draw a house! Yup, you got it, draw another house. Again, don't think too long about it. Just draw it! In the third section, draw a house! We're on a roll. Keep going! In the fourth section, draw a house. I know, another house! In the fifth section, draw a house. Over halfway! You can do it! In the sixth section, draw a house. Seventy-five percent or three quarters of the way there. You're doing a great job! In the seventh section, draw a house! Are you having fun? Don't worry, we're nearly there. In the eighth section, you got it, draw a house!

Don't worry if you're not a Rembrandt or Van Gogh, I'm not either. I never graduated beyond stick men in art. The important thing here is just to draw what comes into your head.

I've done this exercise several times, sometimes when led by other writers and sometimes when I have in turn led groups. The results are always interesting.

When I did this exercise with my Writing for Wellness group most of the houses ended up looking like a series of boxes. There were some variations such as chimneys, pathways, curtains and different doors, but apart from that, the boxes were all the same. We were all well-brought up adults who had been taught to think inside, rather than outside the box. No doubt we had wild imaginations as children, like that of my nephew. but at some point we were taught to be sensible, taught to be realistic, taught to reel in the wild dreams of our imagination and think of life contained within a box with a roof, four windows and a front door.

But, as I have already said, children have unfettered imaginations. Just as my nephew was able to think expansively to bring into being creatures that, as far as we know, do not yet exist in the universe, so too a class of six-year olds were able to think outside the box when faced with the house challenge. Their responses varied wildly. A six-year-old, when asked to draw a house might draw a house boat, a toadstool for a fairy to live in, a treehouse, a tepee, an igloo, a bird's nest, a cave, a spaceship, a submarine, or a plethora of other out of the box ideas. One even drew a picture of a Banana House! Roald Dahl even imagined life in a giant peach!

As we sit down to begin our journey of Writing for Wellness, it's important to give ourselves permission to think outside the box, to dream dreams, and go to places in our imagination that we may not have been to for a very long time.

In order to unlock this in each of us in our group, we began with some simple exercises that would help us explore the world of the imagination. We set up our proverbial sandpits and got down and started to play.

Some of us found this easier than others. Several of the writers said at the beginning that they had no imagination, that they weren't very good at this kind of thing. If that is you, don't worry. What I can tell you is that without fail, sometimes quickly, sometimes slowly, the people in our group have given themselves permission to wonder, pause, reflect, and think well and truly outside the box.

When that happens, it is a privilege and pure delight to see. It's like the flower opening its petals for the first time and turning towards the sun, it's like the smell of petrichor on parched soil after the rain has come, it's like the taste of freshly-brewed coffee in the morning, the sound of a bubbling brook, and the feel of fresh sheets on your bed all rolled into one. Why? Because it's through unlocking the imagination that we get to create, we allow ourselves to dream, and we can start to experience what it truly means to be alive.

Activity Two: The Source of our Imagination

If there was one question, I would have wanted to ask author J.K. Rowling, it would have been, "where do you draw your imagination from to create such complete imaginary worlds?" Thankfully, during a radio interview with the BBC, someone asked that very question, and Rowling answered it. She described a source of water from which her inspiration came, and then a dwelling, or shelter, next to the water in which she worked. She said, and I paraphrase, that you need both inspiration/imagination and discipline/hard work to be able to write. The water for her represents the imagination, the shelter the workspace.

Taking this idea, I asked my group to spend just ten minutes writing about what their body of water might look like and what their workspace dwelling might comprise of. Why don't you have a go now? Set the timer for ten minutes and write, "the water is…" and see what happens next.

Everybody finished? Here's what mine looked like:

> *The water is still, dark and misty. Its depths are unfathomable. I stand on the edge of this vast, intransient lake with its onyx hues and glacial sheen and ponder how I am to draw from it. There are no buckets, nothing that will hold it. If I scoop it up in my hands, it finds every crack in my fingers and disappears from my grasp. I can only wait.*
>
> *I wait, and wait and wait for something to stir, but nothing comes. In despair I stare out across the gloom, squinting into the dark. A gently pulsing orb appears, hovering over the depths, and slowly but surely begins to glide towards me. It comes to rest before my face which is now glowing in its light. My eyes are wide with excitement as I turn, and the orb turns with me.*
>
> *I go inside a beat up old wooden shack with creaky floorboards and dusty shelves. I sit on a rickety chair, on a velvet cushion, and begin to bash away at the keys of an old typewriter. The orb is still before me.*
>
> *Eventually, it dims, the light fades, my eyes grow tired, and I know that it is enough for today. Tomorrow, I will return to my lake and wait.*

How did you get on? The important thing to remember is there are no right or wrongs to these exercises. All your writing to come out of this book is to you, for you and by you. It doesn't pay to compare. Perhaps you'd like to blog or tweet about your experiences. Don't forget to share using the hashtag #writingforwellness.

Activity Three: A Rose by Any Other Name

The next exercise was very simple. We just wrote a list of names. I didn't give any more instructions than this. We simply set the timer for three minutes and started to write. How about you have a go at doing that now.

The results were interesting. All the names written by the people in the group were proper sounding names with established first and last names. Some were the names of real people, or well-known characters from fiction.

I then reset the timer for three minutes and asked them to write a new list of names, but they couldn't use any established names. They found this harder, but eventually their minds and imaginations opened so that names like Blovadec Darwelov and Camarick Bulleroi emerged. Have a go yourself now.

The purpose of all these exercises is to give us permission to think outside the box and dare to imagine.

Activity Four: Going Where No One Has Gone Before

Now we were ready to have some fun, and imagine we were exploring a new planet. Set the timer for ten minutes and describe landing on a planet for the first time. What do you see, what can you hear, how does it smell? For the first time we started to share names and descriptions of worlds and creatures through the eyes of an unfettered six-year-old.

One lady landed on a blue planet where the blue-faced people with buttons for noses had long necks and wore sailor outfits. Another member of the group described a planet that one might believe would have been the setting for the Garden of Eden with lush vegetation, animals that you could communicate with, and where everything lived together in harmony with each other. A third described a somewhat weightless world where the ground was springy, and you could bounce up and down on it like the bouncy castle at the fair.

What would your world look like? I'd love to hear about it. Feel free to share.

Activity Five: Is it a Bird, is it a Plane?

The last activity in this chapter looking at imagination was a five-minute task to imagine that we were a vehicle and to describe the vehicle. This was an interesting one with varied responses from the group members. One was a fighter plane, blasting the enemy virus with missiles, one was a tugboat, hauling supplies along the River Thames, a third was a steam train, painted bright blue, gliding through the English countryside, taking passengers to the sea. If you were a vehicle, what vehicle would you be?

Summary

Imagination is the key that unlocks the door to our authentic selves. As adults, many of us have had our imaginative bubbles burst to the extent that we placed it in straight jacket and wouldn't let it walk free. When we give ourselves permission to wonder, pause and reflect, to think outside the box, it's like watching a flower bloom in the garden of our soul. There are no right or wrongs in the realm of the imagination. All Writing for Wellness is to you, for you and by you. Let us dare to believe that anything is possible as we continue this journey of self-discovery together and let us together watch the flowers grow.

In our next chapter, we'll be looking at the importance of journalling in Writing for Wellness.

2 TOO BUSY NOT TO JOURNAL

When I was a teenager one of the things some of the girls used to say at school was, "Good girls keep diaries; bad girls don't have time." I would suggest that we are too busy not to keep a diary. In this chapter we'll explore the joy of journalling and begin to write a journal ourselves.

My Grandpa's Diaries

One of my passions is family history, and I have spent many hours working on the various branches of my blended family tree. We are incredibly fortunate in that my grandfather kept a diary from the age of fifteen. Reading back over it now, we are treated to a snapshot of life in north east London between the wars.

My great-grandfather was a confectioner and tobacconist. He owned a shop called the Bon Bon on Forest Road in Walthamstow. Grandpa would help in the shop, serving customers, sweeping floors and dressing the windows. He seemed to enjoy the latter the most. When he wasn't working, he'd take his dog Tippy on long walks through the Lee Valley which he described in intricate detail.

There's also this funny tale of my grandfather taking the bus to town to buy a trouser press for his neighbour. Carrying it home on the bus was hilarious, as was the canny mark-up he put on the press which he promptly banked in his savings account. Buy low, sell high, was in my grandfather's blood. He was the consummate salesman.

My Teenage Self

I, myself, kept a diaries throughout the whole of my teens. I look back at them now and laugh at the passion with which I fell in and out of love, with my struggles as a spotty, hormonal teen in 1980s England. I smile at the coloured pens I used, the stumps of tickets to the cinema, concerts, and train journeys to London to shop in Carnaby Street in search of DM boots and tasselled skirts.

Yet despite the gift of distance now, enabling me to laugh and smile, I know that my teens were not always easy times. Sometimes they were acutely painful, whether it be because of an argument with one of my parents, the loss of a boyfriend, or the cruelty of friends. My diary was my constant companion through all of this, ever faithful, never judging, always listening.

Famous Diarists

One of the biggest things I advocate to people wanting to embark on any writing is to become a prolific reader. Books are a massive part of our inspiration well. This is no less true when keeping a diary. There are several famous diarists who are worth a mention here.

Considering the times that we live in, and the fact that we are currently on lock down because of a global pandemic, it is perhaps not surprising that people have been drawing comparisons between the signs of the times and the world depicted in the diary of Samuel Pepys. Pepys' diary covers three important events in British history – the plague, the Great Fire of London, and the coronation of Charles II. I highly recommend giving it a read. I'll always remember the story of him burying his cheese in his garden!

Another famous diarist was Scott of the Antarctic. Captain Scott's expedition to the Antarctic was to prove fatal for him and his men. The juxtaposition of the inward journey when faced with the ravages of the outward journey is striking and powerful, if, at the same time, utterly heart-wrenching. Reading his words at the point when he knows he is going to die give us a snapshot of what is important in life, of how we should come together and focus on what unites us rather than on what divides us, and how we should never let the sun go down on our anger. If you can stomach the inevitability of this work, I recommend you read it. Just make sure you keep a box of tissues next to you as you go.

This brings me on to Virginia Woolf. Another whose life was doomed to be cut short, this time through suicide. Yet Woolf's diaries depict an exciting and creative time during the formation of the Bloomsbury set in London and are a great insight into the workings of the creative mind. Worth picking up.

Finally, and perhaps most famously, is the Diary of Anne Frank. The diary of the fifteen-year-old Dutch girl, hiding from the Germans with her family in an attic in Amsterdam, has sold millions of copies worldwide and has been translated into over forty languages. Justin Bieber was recently criticised for asking whether Anne would have been a Belieber (one of his super fans), whilst on a trip he took to her hiding place. People said it was in poor taste, but I believe it was a very poignant question and hitting on an important point.

Justin was realising that Anne was an ordinary teenage girl in extraordinary circumstances, horrific circumstances, that could happen to anyone if we do not learn the lessons from the past. He was identifying with her. I can too. Anne fancied boys like I did in my teens, she would have had favourite music to listen to just like I did as I sat cross-legged on my bedroom floor making mixer tapes for every occasion. If she had been born today, she might well have been a Belieber, a Directioner or a Harry Potter fan. Through Anne's diaries she becomes accessible to us, real and relatable, and we start to develop empathy as what is human in us connects with what is human in her.

Activity One: Begin Writing a Journal

One of the first "homework" tasks I set the group was to keep a diary. Some members already kept one, ranging from a couple of sentences a day about what they did to lengthy journals about their feelings. But for most of the people in the group this was either a new or ancient endeavour. They found notebooks, journals and diaries to write in. Some even went to town and ordered a new one online, complete with a bouquet of freshly sharpened pencils, a rainbow of gel pens and a shiny new pencil case. There was the excitement and trepidation of going back to school and starting out on a new adventure.

To get them going, I asked them to think about three simple questions:

What did you read or hear in the news which gave you new insight?

With headlines dominated by coronavirus, it was little wonder that news of the pandemic featured heavily here. But people also focussed on other stories that stayed with them, such as the courageous and inspirational walk by Captain Tom Moore who, aged ninety-nine did one hundred laps of his garden to raise over thirty-three million for NHS charities.

Others got creative with their news, subscribing to everything from Henpicked, a site for women over forty, to LadsBible, the title of which gives it away. We had stories that made us laugh out loud, cry buckets, and inspire us, all whilst writing down a little bit of history.

What did you do today?

This question reminds me of the Richard Scarry books I read as a child, which explored how people spent their day, whilst being on the lookout for Lowly Worm. Whether you're a front-line worker, putting your own safety on the line to heal, feed and protect the nation, whether you're an average member of the local community leaving shopping and medicine on people's doorsteps, whether you're a parent home-schooling your children, an elderly or vulnerable person who has to isolate, or someone who is sick and trying to recover, every single one of us has a story to tell that is of value. Our lives matter. What we do all day matters.

If burying a cheese in the back garden during the Great Fire of London becomes a story that is told in history, imagine what people in the future might think of reading about our Zoom meetings, our attempts to sew face masks out of old pillow cases, and our socially-distanced walks in nature. Tell your story. What did you do all day?

How did you feel today?

This can be the hardest question to answer. I know I for one used to spend a lot of time running away from my feelings. They most definitely were not my friend, but rather something to be avoided at all cost. Have you ever watched the Disney film, 'Inside Out?' It is a genius way of helping children access their feelings, and I for one loved it. I'd recommend it.

Once we can trust our feelings enough to cry without thinking we will drown in our tears, to stomp with rage on daily walks without causing an earthquake, to express our fears without succumbing to them, we can start to write them down and they can become our friends, showing us how we are doing, and what we might do in response to them.

One of the other lessons I have learned from keeping a journal all these years is the power of getting thoughts out of my head and on to the page. The more I journal, the less cluttered my head feels, and the more at peace with myself I become. Give it a try and see what you think.

Memorabilia

As I mentioned when talking about my teenage diaries, I look back on them now and smile as memories of past concerts are triggered by tickets I have stuck inside. I've recently started to do this again, although living in lockdown has changed the content. There are no cinema, theatre or concern tickets. Instead, there are pressed flowers, the little notes people send me encouraging me to persevere with my writing, and the letters from family and friends. It could even be the label from a packet of toilet roll, to remind you of the crazy stockpiling that went on in the early days of lock down. Memorabilia is a tangible element of journalling, along with doodles, photos and the like. They add a third dimension to your writing and trigger memories when you come back to them later.

Other ways to Journal

If you'd prefer not to write your journals down, there are other ways to record your thoughts and feelings. As some of you may be aware, I have been recording a Staycation Podcast during this time which is exploring my own thoughts and feelings during life in lockdown. You may not want to publish your recordings online, but it can be both fun and freeing to record your journal in this way.

Summary

There is no right or wrong way to journal. All journalling is to you, for you and by you. The important thing is that it is a joy and a gift to yourself. Buy yourself a nice new notebook or journal, even invest in some fun new pens and a pencil case, try to write every day, even if it's just one sentence. Don't try and catch up on missed days.

You can use the prompts above, but there are many others. Think of some of your own and don't be afraid to step outside the box. You are beautiful and this journal can be a beautiful reflection of you too, helping you process things, and getting things out of your head and on to the page. There are no limits. Just begin and see where it takes you.

In the next chapter we will explore what it means to be a Lady of Letters.

3 LADIES OF LETTERS

When I was in junior school, somewhere between the ages of ten and eleven, my teacher brought in some forms for us to fill out. We were given the opportunity of selecting countries in the world where we would be matched up with a corresponding child so that we could become pen pals. Two of my pairings wrote me a letter, one girl in Burgos, Spain, and another in Zagreb in what was the former Yugoslavia.

I can't tell you how overjoyed I was to receive my letters, and how diligently I replied to them. I still have them to this day. I keep a cedar chest at the end of my bed for all my keepsakes. This chest is full of letters, postcards, recorders, name badges, certificates, small items of clothing and the like. The letters are the best.

Even when friends from school moved away, we kept in contact with each other by writing letters back and forth. Every time I made a new friend on holiday, we would exchange addresses at the end and begin to correspond. Boyfriends would write me letters even though they would see me regularly, friends would pass notes in class. I have these treasures to look back on fondly and I am very grateful that I grew up in an age where something tangible could be kept reminding me of days gone by.

I am adopted. Through an absolute miracle I was reunited with my birth mother and her family when I was just shy of eighteen. We began by corresponding, and she agreed that she would write me the first letter. The sense of anticipation and delight I felt on hearing the thud of envelopes on the doormat and rushing down to see bright stickers on the seal is beyond description. I rushed upstairs to have a read.

I have poured over the pages of that miraculous letter so many times that I can almost quote it chapter and verse. My mother is a beautiful narrator and a wordsmith in ways I can only hope to aspire to. In those pages she re-introduced me to my long-lost family in America and my heart was, and is, bursting with gratitude for the utter joy our reunion has become.

I come from a family of letter writers. My aunt, my grandmother, my grandfather and cousin have all written me beautiful prose over the years. They encompass a large section of my keepsake chest, which, incidentally, came from them anyway. My English family also love to correspond, and I have a selection of cards, notes and letters from them when I was away at university and afterwards went to live in America.

Now I love technology. Having friends and family scattered all over the world I am hugely appreciative of the tools I can pick up to be able to easily stay in contact with them all wherever they are. I also appreciate the advent of the smart phone, which basically acts as my brain these days. But what has saddened me as a result of all the progress we've been making is that culturally we have started to lose the knack of writing things down, corresponding with each other by hand, and having tangible words to hold on to when people are gone.

A while back I wrote a blog post entitled, 'RSVP and the Death of the Notecard,' in which I spoke about the shifting sands of cultural norms where even if you create an event on Facebook, which might well be catered and therefore needing reasonably firm numbers, people hit the maybe button without giving it a second thought. Equally, when was the last time you received a thank you note, or a thinking of you card, after an event you hosted or when you were going through a difficult time?

But all is not lost, all is not doom and gloom, there is a re-emergence of letter-writing and note-taking that is sweeping across the UK and the rest of the Western World. People are purchasing delightful, coloured notepaper, fanciful stickers, a bouquet of pens and sparkly pencil cases. They are investing in nibbed-pens, bottles of coloured ink, and they are starting to reignite their passion for letters.

On the third week of our Writing for Wellness group I gave the members a task. We all drew names out of a hat and then I challenged them to write a letter to that person over the coming week. Those that did not have supplies found packets of paper, envelopes, stickers, pens and stamps left on their doorsteps, along with their usual food and medicine deliveries. We were up and ready to become Ladies of Letters once again.

The person whose name I drew was a friend of some other group members that I had got to know through my Monday morning knitting group. I was so excited to get her name so that I could write and thank her for all her encouragement, and enthusiastic participation in the group. She is an absolute gem and has a beautifully evocative way of describing a scene so that you are transported there in the moment. It was such a joy to write to her.

I got a letter from Felicity. Felicity has a beautiful spirit, is very funny, very kind and generous, and very wise. She cut her paper out into the shape of a heart (did I also mention very creative?) and sent it to me that way inside a card. Her words were very moving indeed and her letter, once I have finished reading it over and over, will take pride of place in my keepsake chest.

The other members of the group fed back that they too had thoroughly enjoyed receiving their letters and reading them. It brought joy to their week and over the weeks more letters and cards have been sent back and forth between the members of the group. I suspect that so long as we don't cram our lives full of business after lockdown is over, this is a habit that will continue.

Now it's time for you to have a go. Here are some activities for you to try. Don't forget to let me know how it goes.

Activity One: Letters in Lockdown

If you can, write a handwritten letter to someone and post it to them. Don't worry if you haven't got fancy paper or coloured pens. The important thing is to write to them. Tell them what you've been doing. Ask them what they have been doing. Tell them what they mean to you. Perhaps you can agree with some others that you know to be pen pals. I hope you have as much joy as we have had in receiving letters from each other at this time.

If you can't get out of the house, don't worry! Still hand-write your letter, but then take a photo of it and e-mail it to the person. They can still print out your hand-written letter at the other end and peruse it over a cup of tea.

Activity Two: Letter to Your Teenage Self

I've done this exercise with a few groups in the past. It's very simple. Write a letter as the adult you are today to your teenage self. What would you want to say to the teenage you? How would you want to encourage yourself? How might you reassure yourself? In what ways might you warn yourself about potential pitfalls and obstacles along the journey of your life? How might you forgive yourself?

This was quite an emotional experience for several people in my group. You never know where something might land. Different people have had strong reactions to different activities at different times. It's seemingly random, but there is a pervading sense that the God of the universe is somehow holding us all together, carrying us through, and providing us with the tissues when we need to have a good cry.

Coming together week on week in this group has been like a giant hug in the middle of social distancing. It has felt like a strong hand, holding us as we walk through the dark, not knowing when the light will come at the end. Taking part in the group and doing the activities together, we've been able to unlock the door, in a safe, loving and encouraging environment, to the sorrows of the past, to our hopes and dreams for the future, as we sit with ourselves in the present knowing that we are beautifully made, truly loved, and are absolutely free.

Activity Three: Letter Between Characters

Remember those lists of names, both real and imagined, that I got you to make at the start of your journey through this book? Now's the time to pull them back out again. For this activity we're going to be writing a letter between two people, but first, we're going to explore a little bit about them.

Begin by selecting one of the names that jumps out at you from your list. Set your timer for three minutes and describe the character that you think belongs to that name. What do they look like, how do they speak and walk? What are the good things about their personality? What are their defects of character? Where do they fit in the world? What do they do all day?

After your first three minutes, do the same for a second name on your list. At the end of six minutes you should have two rough sketches of the characters that go with two names. Now on to the fun part. Write a letter from one of your characters to the other character. It can be about whatever you like. Share it with your group or share it online.

Mine was a letter to Lila May Dawson, an American socialite, in her 60s, who had recently moved to Somerset. The letter is from James Beauchamp, a man in his 50s who wears corduroy trousers and a mustard sweater that his mother brought him for Christmas. James is President of the local horticultural society.

Dear Ms Dawson,

I am writing to inform you that your application to join the Little Gatesby Horticultural Society denied and that your entry in the recent, 'best orchid from cutting,' competition at the summer fete, for which you were awarded first prize, had been disqualified and we would be obliged if you would return the silver cup to us at your earliest convenience.

I would like to take the opportunity to remind you of the honour code you signed on entering which clearly stated that the entry should have been from a cutting. You were seen, Ms Dawson, by Mrs Marchmont, at the garden centre, purchasing said orchid, and Mrs Willis happened to notice the tags you cut off in your bins just after the fete.

I don't know how things are done in America, Ms Dawson, but here in England that is simply not cricket and very poor show indeed.

Sincerely,
James G Beauchamp, Esq.

Summary

Writing and receiving hand-written letters can be an absolute joy and delight and a very good way to bring a little light into your own life, and the lives of others, during the dark days of lockdown. Despite the wonders of modern technology, nothing beats being able to keep something that a loved one or friend has touched, and the thought that goes into the words on the page are to be treasured forever.

Whether it be letters from pen pals as a child, friends that have since moved away, long-lost or distant family, or just a quick RSVP or a note to say thank you, there is no doubt that there is a rebirth of the love of writing by hand, and more men and women across the world are becoming Ladies and Men of Letters once again. I encourage you to join their merry band and be a Lady of Letters or a Man of Musings yourself.

In the next chapter we'll be looking at the power of memory joggers.

4 MEMORY JOGGERS

When embarking on a Writing for Wellness journey, using different tools to unlock memories is a useful way to examine how we are doing today, how we feel about the past, and what we are bringing with us into the future. Memory joggers can come in a wide variety of forms, they can use props, they can use the imagination, and they can encompass all the senses. They can even sometimes tap into our sixth sense, or intuition.

I have used memory jogger exercises scattered throughout the meetings of our Writing for Wellness group. It is important to provide variety as we meet for two hours with a short break in the middle. Some of the exercises are light and joyful, others dig a little deeper. We don't work our way through the exercises as they are written out chapter by chapter in this book. Instead we dip into different kinds of exercises at different times and in different ways. Memory joggers are just one of those ways.

Activity One: Ice Cream

The use of the imagination in triggering memories is a great way to have fun and play. It's often when we spend time in the fantasy world that we give ourselves permission to explore feelings and thoughts that in the cold light of day we would keep firmly under lock and key.

Set your timer for five minutes and write the word ice-cream at the top of the page. Now write about ice-cream for five minutes. Don't think too hard about it. If it leads you off on tangents, allow yourself to go there. The important thing is to keep the pen moving no matter what comes out. Even if all you do is attempt to name every flavour of ice-cream you have ever tasted, that's perfectly ok. Go with the flow so to speak. Come back when your time is up!

Done? How was it for you? Where did your writing about ice-cream take you? Did it remind you of childhood holidays at the seaside? Did it inspire you to try new flavours? Did it unlock something else for you?

When I did this exercise with the Writing for Wellness group, it was absolutely fascinating to see the responses. One lady doesn't like ice-cream, so her writing began with explaining why, and then lead on to a diatribe of all the other things in her life that she doesn't like. She found it very cathartic to get it all out of her head and on to the page.

Another lady described her childhood holidays and got very choked up as she thought about happy days gone by and loved ones lost. This exercise has inspired her to think about writing a book about her family to pass on to future generations. She is now rummaging through boxes of photos and flipping through old albums and having an absolute whale of a time.

A third group member ended up writing an hilarious tale about ice cream which could equal that of Charlie and the Chocolate Factory any day, and I've been encouraging her to expand on it and consider writing a children's book. Who would have thought where the seemingly simple subject of ice-cream would take us? Where has it taken you? I'd love to hear.

Activity Two: It Helped that I Cried

Thinking back on specific events in our lives can also be a useful memory jogger. The next exercise that I want to talk about is one I gave the group quite early on in their journey together. I asked them to describe their first concert.

True to form, there was one lady who doesn't like music, so this was an excruciating description of a thoroughly unhappy experience of her being a captive audience. None-the less, she wrote it with wit and vivacity and thoroughly entertained us all.

Others, in contrast, were reminded of how joyful an experience it was, and how much they valued listening to live music. They planned to seek out live music after lockdown, are regular followers of Gary Barlow's Crooner sessions, and the collaborations between Andrew Lloyd Webber, Lin-Manuel Miranda and others. They are even joining me in an online Mama Mia party amongst friends this weekend.

About Mama Mia, my first concert was to see ABBA on my seventh birthday. This is what I wrote about it:

My party was over, and my friends had gone home. Streamers and empty cups were strewn across the table as we settled down in front of the television. A news item came on announcing that ABBA were playing at Wembley Arena that very night and that tickets were still available. I begged and begged and begged to go. My mum, my grandma Margaret and I piled into the Mini Clubman and we made the short journey to Wembley.

We stood in the queue to get tickets but the people in front of us got the last ones. I was hysterical. So near and yet so far. There was a quiet discussion between the adults and two tickets were purchased from touts at exorbitant prices.

Tears of joy now ran down my face as mum took my hand and we all walked to the ticket barrier. Something was said to the security guard and he crouched down, so we were eyeball to eyeball.

"You're going to be a good girl and sit on your mother's knee, aren't you?"

I nodded obediently, the tears still glistening in my eyes.

The next thing I knew, he lifted me up and over the turnstile and mum and grandma piled in behind me. We were all going to get to see the concert!

I still remember where we sat, stage left, about halfway up. They sang all my favourite songs. I didn't sit on my mother's lap. I stood and danced and sang too. Their costumes, the music, the lights, the smiling faces, filled me with joy to over brimming.

I hate to admit it, but I started to get tired towards the end. We began to make our way out as Thank You for the Music was played. I was the girl with golden hair, but I was also seven, had been at my own birthday party, it was late, and I was exhausted. The tears began to flow again, simply because of fatigue. I knew it was a day to remember and here I am, forty years later, writing about it like it was yesterday.

We got back to the car and pulled away from the stadium to go home. As we pulled up at a roundabout, we came beside a limousine. I'm sure ABBA were inside. How they got out of the stadium so quickly I do not know but they must have left immediately after coming off stage. I waved at them and imagined them waving back.

I was quiet for the journey home, thinking about what had happened that day. I remembered the face of the security guard before her lifted me over the barrier.

"I'm glad I cried," I said quietly.

Activity Three: Museum Exhibit

Another exercise using the imagination is to imagine that there is going to be a museum exhibit of your life and to think of one object that might be in that exhibit. Describe the object and the sign that might accompany it.

The wonderful thing about this one was that the group members went searching around their homes for their objects so that they could look at them while they wrote about them and could show us the objects when they shared their writing. Tangible prompts and props like this can really help us dig into our memories and talk about our feelings.

An alternative to this could be to find an item in your kitchen that started life in someone else's kitchen and to write about that. What memories it has, where it has been, in whose hands it has been.

Back to the museum piece. We had candlesticks from grandparents, favourite books, pieces of craft work, silver spoons and even a pair of baby shoes. This exercise has inspired one lady to write a history of her life in objects with photographs of them all, to share with her children.

Activity Four: The First Kiss

This activity got us thinking about a specific time in our past. I suggest you set the timer for five minutes and write about your own first kiss. Where and when was it? What were you wearing? What was the other person wearing? What sights, smells, touch and taste did you experience? What could you hear? Was it the sound of your own heart beating faster?

People interpreted this exercise differently. Some talking about the kiss from their mothers when they were small babies. Others talked about a parent kissing it better when they had a scrape on their knee as a small child. Others still talked about the sloppy kiss from an ageing aunt at Christmas. But the majority went the expected and traditional route of their first romantic kiss as a teenager. Mine sounded like the pages of a Mills and Boon novel, and I've printed an extract of it here.

> "His name was Juan Carlos and he was the best-looking boy on the Costa del Sol. I was thirteen, and my sister and I had gone to a party on the beach. Sardines were being cooked over an open fire and Sangria flowed from buckets in the sand. We made eye contact, and he asked if we could go for a walk alone along the shore. Hand in hand we walked, the gentle waves encircling our ankles.
> We found a sun-lounger further up the beach and sat down, my head on his shoulder as the sun set on the horizon. He turned my face to his and our lips met as I melted into him."

Activity Five: Portraits Through Time

The last memory jogger exercise I'm going to talk about here involves photographs. At the end of a meeting I gave the ladies some homework. I asked them to find three photographs of themselves at different ages in their life and to bring them to the group the following week. Nearly all the married members brought a wedding photo as part of the mix. We began with the earliest photo and they spent time describing who they were at that age, not just what they looked like but everything about their character and circumstances.

We wrote about all three photos in turn. This time, the writing produced a strong emotional reaction in some as they had forgotten what was going on for them at the time the photos were taken. One remembered their father had died and had not been able to give them away at their wedding. Another's first picture was of themselves as a young child sitting on their beloved grandmother's knee, and when they came to write about it, the happy memories of an idyllic childhood spent with this woman brought tears to their eyes.

Not all the photographs brought up happy memories. One seemingly happy photograph of a young girl coming out of the water at the beach on holiday brought up memories of an unhappy school year that preceded it when the girl had been on the receiving end of bullying. You never know what is going to come up in our writing and when something as powerful as that emerges, we give the person all the time they need, and no one is under any pressure to share if they don't want to. We are all here to listen to and support one another but we are never here to fix. That is for the professionals.

Remember the lady who got excited by the museum exhibit exercise? As you can probably imagine, this was right up her street. She had already been spending time rummaging through old photographs and she brought more than three with her to this gathering. As people started to talk about writing memoirs, family histories, romance, mysteries, children's books and poetry, I suggested that we begin a second writing group for the creative writers amongst us who would like to write with a view to publishing. This is how the Shenley Writers group was formed. It is going strong and we are even having conversations about the possibility of starting a literary festival every year in the Shenley Walled Garden.

Summary

Using memory joggers in our Writing for Wellness can help reconcile us to the past, empower us in the present, and face the future with optimism and joy. Memory joggers can take many forms, whether they be a random subject, a specific event, an object, or a photograph. These exercises can be intense, so it's recommended that they be scattered about amongst your writing group, interspersed with some lighter tasks.

You never know where they are going to lead. For some, it may bring up happy memories of days gone by, for others it might help them understand their likes and dislikes more. For others still it might mean they remember something painful and need some extra help and support to process. It might even lead some to explore writing for publication, and who knows, we may yet have more literary festivals spring up around the country in the aftermath of this lockdown.

In the next chapter, we will start to explore the way sound can prompt our writing.

5 SOUNDS AND SILENCE

One thing we spent quite a bit of time on in our Writing for Wellness group were different forms of audible prompts. We spend so much time talking about what we see, and rarely talk about what we hear. One of the things I have noticed more since we went into lockdown is the beautiful birdsong right outside my window. I am fortunate in that I live on a hill surrounded by stunning views and beautiful countryside. Just outside my bedroom window is a majestic oak tree and from its branches every morning I hear the dawn chorus, ably lead by a proud and vocal blackbird. There are many ways to use audible prompts and we are going explore some of them in this chapter. You might find some of your own.

Activity One: The Sound of Silence

The first time we looked at audible prompts I surprised the group by asking them to bring ear plugs and / or noise-cancelling headphones. Many of them had partners who snored so there was ample supply. I then got them to cancel out all noise around themselves and write about what the sound of silence meant to them. You try it now.

One thing that happened is that we very quickly lost all track of time. We started to write and forgot where we were and became immersed in our own thoughts. We eventually, after much hilarity of gestures and waving, came back together to share.

For some, silence came thick and heavy. These people didn't like the idea of being alone, and the silence made them feel vulnerable. Whether they lived by themselves or with others, they would normally have sound in their lives, whether it be the radio, television or an audio book. To sit in silence and write was excruciating for them. They didn't want to be there.

They became angry and belligerent in their writing, the inner child voicing its grief and despair. Fear was often at the heart of it all and this exercise gave them the opportunity to explore their loneliness and fears and to begin to be comfortable in their own company.

One lady, the philosopher amongst us, looked at silence in the abstract, and discussed the tree falling in the wood debate and whether sound was only sound if there was someone or something to hear it. She also talked about the silence to be found in the cosmos, how there is no sound in space. Perhaps we are uncomfortable with this, and instead fill our films with the evocative and uplifting scores by John Williams and the bleeps and zooms of the special effects team.

For many, silence was a welcome friend. These group members are, overall, comfortable in their own skin. They are the mindfulness crowd, the yogis of this world, the contemplatives who embrace silence and use the time to breathe, recharge, and allow their thoughts to float by in front of them without trying to stop them.

I am now one of those who calls silence my friend. I never used to be. In the past, silence was to be feared, like the first day our parent kisses us goodbye at nursery and leaves us to our own devices. Like the realisation that we've been shoved out into the spotlight on an empty stage, barely able to remember our lines, with an expectant audience just yards in front of us. Like a viewing platform from a tall building where we look down and realise just how high we've climbed, and our body suddenly starts to imagine what would happen if we fell.

I don't feel like this anymore, and I have Writing for Wellness to partially thank for it. There is serenity and peace to be found in its branches, there's relaxation to be seen in its limbs, there's food for the soul to be found in its leaves. Silence is indeed golden, and as you continue to write it out, it is my sincere hope that one day it will be golden for you too.

Activity Two: Everyday Sounds

On another week we began to look at everyday sounds. I asked the group to record an everyday sound on their phones from one week to the next. Their choices were interesting in and of themselves. One lady recorded the sound of a bath draining its water, including the final sucking sound as the whirlpool disappears down the plughole. Another recorded the sound of a lawnmower in the garden with its rhythmic hum and the crackle and snap when it hit a stone or twig. A third recorded the sound of a kettle boiling and a mug being filled to make tea.

Each of these sounds was recorded, and then they played it back and wrote about what they were hearing. When we got back together again, we read our descriptions to one another. Everyone succeeded in evoking the sounds they wrote about. We heard the suck of the water down the drain, the low hum of the mower, the sharp crack as the blade it a twig, gathering churning of the water boiling in a kettle and the hiss as it is poured out like lungs expelling air after holding your breath, the clink of a spoon and the thud of a fridge door.

Hearing is the last sense to leave us when we die, yet it is also the last sense we talk about when we write. As the group began to work through these audio exercises, they began to appreciate this sense so much more, and started to become grateful for the thud of letters on the doormat in the morning, the giggles and shouts of children playing in their gardens, and even the snoring of their husbands or partners. Mind you, they were also thankful for the ear plugs and the sound that silence brings.

Activity Three: On the Move

This activity was another piece of homework I set for the ladies. Once more they were asked to record something and then write about it and bring it back to the group. This time, I asked them to record the sounds around them as they went on their daily health walks. I suggest you do it when you go out today. Whether it be in the car, walking, cycling, or on the bus or train, the sounds around us when we are on the move are fascinating.

I don't know if it was because I was intentionally recording the sound, but when I did this on my walk it felt as if the birdsong down in Cow Banks Wood was louder than it had ever been before and the hum of bees as they lighted from bloom to bloom, stuffing their pockets with the nectar until their wings ached and they made their way home to the hive almost became a part of me as I felt more at one with nature.

> The wind rustled in the trees, a small mammal, possibly a rabbit, scratched around in the undergrowth to my right and a woodpecker hammered into a trunk to find its lunch. I also noticed the sounds I didn't hear. I couldn't hear the low hum of the M25 motorway in the distance. I wasn't interrupted by the loud squeal of jet planes overhead; I didn't even pass another human being on the path that day. Everything I heard was natural, at one with each other, nothing jarring, nothing mechanical, nothing to interrupt. As I sat on a decaying, fallen branch, and took out my notebook to write, I too felt a part of the scene and as my spirit, my soul, my lifeforce began to connect with the lifeforces that were around me, I began to appreciate in a deeper and more profound way than I ever had before just how great it was to be part of something bigger than myself. No longer was I an island. No longer was I alone and afraid. I belonged, I had a part to play, I was free.

The reactions from the other members of the group as we shared our experiences were varied. Some took a comical approach to the sounds as they examined them for the first time and found great humour in their description. Others allowed their imaginations to run riot and their writing took them to faraway shores or distant memories. Others, like me, began to feel more present to themselves and the universe than they had ever done before. They could see the beauty of the creation that is around them, they could feel that they are a part of it, and in one moment they could know that they are beautiful too – fearfully and wonderfully made.

Activity Four: Music to Write By

In this last activity I introduced music to our Writing for Wellness group for the first time. You can use any piece of music you like, but I would suggest the first time you do this you don't pick your favourite song or a piece of music you are extremely familiar with. As much as I love to write to the Harry Potter soundtrack, play U2 when I am knitting, or dance to ABBA when I am doing household chores, for the purposes of this exercise it's good to use something where we don't know what to expect next.

I chose Holst's Saturn. I am more familiar with Mars and Jupiter than I am with Saturn. I would have liked to listen to Jupiter instead, and imagine a Welsh choir singing, "I Vow to thee My Country," but Saturn it was. I recommend you give it a go. Just go where the pen takes you and see what happens. Here is my contribution that I shared with the group:

> *"Creeping, crawling, closer and closer, nearer and nearer. Is it going to fall in? Am I going to fall in? I'm getting heavier and heavier but just as I reach the edge, I spread my wings and glide out across the vast expanse, high, high above it all. I can see everything. It all makes perfect sense.*
>
> *Things are moving quickly. Green shoots coming up from cracked soil, poking up and up, uncurling their leaves to bask in the sun, forming buds that explode into a riot of colour. A blanket of grass emerges as a spring of water spirts up from the centre leaving a trail of greenery in its wake.*
>
> *But an army of fire is coming, and a bell rings out. Panic ensues, people dart about in every direction, unsure of where to go. The flames die down and a rabbit hops across the field.*
>
> *A boat floats lazily down the stream. There's a prairie, horses cantering across as I fly up and down around them. Floating on the currents I land on a high nest. I am an eagle."*

As I have already mentioned, one lady doesn't like music, so this wasn't the exercise for her. Despite this, her writing was incredible and highly imaginative. The same was true for the other members of the group. How did you get on? Did you use Saturn or another piece of music? I'd love to hear from you and for you to share what you wrote about.

Summary

Sounds are the last thing we hear and at the same time the last thing we write about. Exploring the role of sounds in our lives can help us tap into our imaginations, evoke our memories, explore our dreams, and help us to become connected to the rest of creation more than we have ever felt before.

Working our way through these exercises, exploring the sound of silence and what it means to be comfortable with our own company and in our own skin, is a powerful tool on the road to Wellness. Exploring everyday sounds like the emptying of a bath, the hum of a lawnmower or the boiling of a kettle can help us become much more present to ourselves, to live in the moment, and to appreciate the small things in life. Writing to music can take us on inner and outer journeys full of adventure to heights we have never imagined we would reach, and to depths we have never explored.

In the next chapter, we will look at a series of, "what ifs…" imagining possibilities beyond our wildest dreams.

6 WHAT IFS…

This chapter explores the exercises the group worked on where we gave ourselves the opportunity to explore what life would be like if… These writings took us into the realm of infinite possibilities, they gave us permission to dream dreams, and they helped us to make plans, amid life after lockdown.

We began with some fun, simple, list-making exercises and slowly built up from there going from the sublime to the ridiculous and everything in between. As with all these chapters, throughout our life in lockdown, as we met online from week to week, we dipped in and out of them, trying different things at different times. I always did my best to read the room and go where they wanted to go, explore what they wanted to explore. The amazing thing about all of this, is that when you create space, you find the space to create, and out of that comes infinite possibilities.

Activity One: My Numbers Came In

How many of you have ever said, "If I win the lottery, I'll…"? We started with this list because it's an easy way to think about what life might be like if our circumstances were different. We set the timer for just three minutes and wrote a list. How about you have a go at doing that now?

There were the usual responses, like paying off the mortgage, retiring early, going on nice holidays, buying a car etc, as well as various donations to charities. But there were also some unique and interesting ones that reflected on the author's personality and heartfelt wants and desires. One man wanted to start an animal sanctuary, another to start homesteading, a third to open a sweet shop. One even wanted to buy a ticket to Mars where she would love to emigrate one day!

Perhaps the most beautiful list of all was by the lady who left her list blank. She honestly couldn't think of anything she wanted in the world that money could buy. This wasn't because she was being difficult, or lacked imagination in any way, it was simply because she was more than content with her lot in life and didn't feel like she wanted or needed anything more. This list was the most profound of all and left us all pondering why some are satisfied with our lives, while others have a thirst for something we do not yet have.

That's not to say that all of us with our expansive list of things we would buy if we won the lottery are somehow missing something in our lives. To write this list can simply be a useful way to decide what is important to us, and to help us discover that what we think is impossible is in fact possible.

Activity Two: Bucket List

The same can be said when we wrote our Bucket Lists. Have you ever written a bucket list before? It's basically a list of things we would like to do before we kick the bucket, before we move on to the next world, cross the rainbow bridge, reach heaven, before we die. If you've never written a bucket list before have a go at writing one now. Don't hold back. Be as expansive and daring as you like. If you have written one before, see if you can find it. Have you done any of the things on your list? Do you have anything new to add?

Here's mine:

Publish a book – yay! I'll be crossing this one off soon!!!
Go for a cruise on the Nile
Walk along the Great Wall of China
Visit the Salt Lakes of Bolivia
Write a novel while staying in Tuscany with other writers
Buy a home in the Cotswolds
Ride a horse along the Camino de Santiago de Compostela
Go to the Holy Land and eat fish by the Sea of Galilee
Get married
Own a horse
Visit St Petersburg and the Winter Palace
See the Northern Lights
Meet J.K. Rowling
Have afternoon tea with the Queen
Be interviewed by Oprah
Be able to get out of the house and go for a drive
Have a swimming pool at home

Before lockdown I think my list would have looked a lot different. I don't know that my desire to travel and see the world would have been anything like it is today. These are all long-term goals and dreams. Except one. Getting in my car and going for a drive made it on my bucket list. Getting out and seeing friends, family and just somewhere different made it on nearly all the bucket lists in the group. Even the lady who had nothing to list in the previous exercise talked about her desire to see her grandson again and watch him grow into a young man.

What does your list look like? Do you think that life in lockdown has changed your perspective on things? Are there some things you can begin to do, to work towards making some of those dreams a reality? What will your life look like after lockdown? How will it have changed?

Activity Three: Seeing the World from a Difference Place

When I was young, I would sometimes lie at the foot of my stairs, my legs stretched upwards, and gaze up at the ceiling, imagining what life would be like to live upside-down. One important way in which we can begin to write for wellness is to start to see the world from a different place, a new perspective, or even walk a mile in someone else's shoes. Like going on a trip to distant lands, when we return home to our normal lives the time away gives us a fresh perspective and an opportunity to incorporate some of what we have learned along the way.

The same can be said for life in lockdown. Suddenly, all our expectations of what life would be like for us in 2020 vanished as we watched with increasing trepidation and fear as the pandemic spread across the globe. Some of the hardest lessons we have learned are that life is fleeting, we can't take loved ones for granted, and that our day to day existence will never be completely the same as it was before.

But there are some positives to be drawn from our experiences in lockdown, and this was an opportunity for our group to think about those things. We began by spending some time writing about what we loved about our lives before lockdown. I suggest you begin by doing the same. We wrote about the times we got to spend with friends and family. We wrote about the delicious meals out that we enjoyed not having to prepare. We wrote of the museums and great country houses that we had been to. We described the holidays we had been on and the parties we had shared.

We then wrote about what we hadn't liked before lockdown, how stressed we had been, how little time we had, and how we had attempted to approach life by cramming as much into it as possible so that we left no time at all to smell the roses.

We then took some time to write about what we love about life in lockdown. We wrote of our increased awareness of nature around us, the joys of spring and seeing the flowers bloom, of the birdsong, the ability to spend quality time with others in our households and with those whom we were meeting online. We enjoyed the slower pace, the ability to pick up a book and read, to go for leisurely walks, to sit on the phone with a friend.

So, where does this leave us in life after lockdown? What kind of world would we like to step out into? We wrote about what kind of world we would like to live in moving forwards, a world where we had time to stop and be still, where we felt more present in the moment, where our stresses were diminished, and our joys were expanded. We wrote about a world where we not only connected with nature, but also with each other in new and profound ways. We wrote about the power of a hug, the touch of a hand, the smile on the face of a stranger. We dreamed of a world that would learn the lessons of lockdown and step out into a more beautiful and less frazzled existence. What would that world look like for you? How might you take small steps towards making it a reality?

Activity Four: On Distant Shores

For our next activity we used an online random country generator and each of us was given a country to imagine living in. We wrote about the sounds, sights, smells and tastes of our lives in these places as we pictured a different kind of life lived abroad.

Half a dozen of us were either born in another country or had already spent a significant period of time living abroad. But none-the-less, because of the randomness of the selection, the results were delightful. How about you have a go too? Don't cheat and keep selecting until you get your favourite country. I know I would have loved to have picked Italy for the scenery, the wine, the fashions and the food, but someone else had that pleasure and instead, I got...

FINLAND!

I was excited about this. I have a Finnish friend who often describes what her life was like before she moved to the UK. I also saw the disastrous episode of The Apprentice where the teams had to create adverts for the Finnish Tourist Board. Facepalm. What would my life be like in Finland?

It would involve log cabins, roaring fires, Nordic sweaters and socks, lots of craftwork, hot tubs, cross country skiing through pine forests and sweating it out in a sauna. It would also include lots of delicious pastries and other foods, dinners with friends by candlelight and curling up with a good book and a snuggly cat. It might even involve sitting at a small desk in front of an ancient typewriter, churning out pages of my latest novel.

What country did you get? What did you write about? Did it make you want to visit, or even perhaps move there one day? When we focus on the positive in the "other" it gives us an opportunity to expand our horizons and to grow as we go.

Activity Five: Is It a Bird? Is it a Plane?

The next activity was a bit of fun. I asked the group to imagine that they had a superpower, any superpower. It didn't have to be one we had already seen in a film or comic. It could have been something completely new.

You try it now. If you could have any superpower you liked, no matter what it might be, what would that superpower be? Write it down at the top of your page and set your timer for five minutes. Begin writing about life with that superpower. Don't worry where the words go, don't stop yourself if you go off on a tangent. Let yourself be led.

Once we had finished our five minutes we came back together and started to share our writing with each other. Some of us wanted to fly like an eagle, others to be able to move objects like Mary Poppins did, others wanted to be able to instantly teleport themselves to another place, if they had family living far and wide. One writer, who struggles with arthritis, wanted to have superhuman strength to be able to combat the weakness they are experiencing in their hands as they grew older.

Not all of us wanted a superpower per se. We didn't want to fly, teleport or to be able to move objects across a room without touching them. These writers, I among them, wanted instead to be able to hone and refine the gifts and skills that we already had.

I started to write about the gift of intuition, the ability to know the unknowable, to have instincts. When we are living in a much quieter world where the pace of life is slower, our ability to hear our intuition is amplified.

About a year ago I was having a conversation with one of my doctors. We'd dealt with the business of the day and had fallen into a casual conversation for the remainder of my appointment, discussing such things as climate change and over-population. I said to my doctor, "you know, the planet has a way of fighting back." My doctor said, "what do you mean?" and I said, "I think we're due a global pandemic within the next year."

Less than a year later, that global pandemic occurred. Did I make it happen? No, of course not. Did I fully understand the implications of it? Absolutely not. Did I know how I would react to it, or how many people I knew would die? No. Would I have preferred that my prophecy had not come true? You bet.

But in that moment as I was having that conversation in April of 2019, I saw with clarity the direction in which we were heading. I don't know why or how. I just had a sense, and as I thought about it, it made complete sense. That's the gift that I wrote about honing and refining, the ability to see the sign of the times. It's not always convenient, and sometimes it can be overpowering. Any gift, skill or superpower should have the ability to have an on and off switch!

Instead of having a superpower, if you were to hone and refine one of the gifts or skills that you already have, what would it be? Would you like to become an expert listener, a confident speaker, or a proficient writer? Would you like to be able to go from couch to 10k? What might you do to improve something that you already know you can do in your life?

One of the reasons I set out to write this book was because my editor challenged me to just publish. I have spent the last twelve years attempting to write a novel and I'm still working on it. I haven't given up. The only problem has been that I want it to be perfect. I've written it about four times over, about seventy-thousand words each time and every time I've done so I've ended up deleting it.

Now I know that you fellow writers out there will be horrified to hear about this waste of words. But the internal critic in me has won the day, time and again, in the relentless and futile pursuit of perfection.

So, my editor said to me, "just write anything and get it out there and publish it." I'd been thinking for some time about the possibility of sharing with everybody the experiences that we have had in our Writing for Wellness group and I thought, why not tell that story? The story of the writers that got together in lockdown and went on a journey even though they couldn't leave their own homes. I thought one plus side is that I would be under pressure to write this story as quickly as possible. It's topical, it's poignant, it's relevant to today, and it may not be quite so relevant later. So, I had the gift of that deadline built in that I may not have had under other circumstances. I also knew that it would be relatively short and so wouldn't take me too terribly long to write. I made the decision to simply write it, and not care how good it was. Although I planned to edit it, if there was the odd typo or slightly clumsy phrase in it, I would let it go and accept the fact that it was good enough and that it would land where it may.

The single most important thing right now is to get it out there and published. Once I have done that, I can spend the rest of my life as a published author, honing and refining the craft that is writing.

So, what is the thing that brings you the most amount of joy and excitement in your life? What gets your going? What makes you feel most alive? Chase it. Pursue it. Develop it. Hone it and let it become the very superpower that you long for.

Activity Six: If I Could Turn Back Time

The most recent "What If…" we looked at was to ask ourselves the question what if I could turn back time? I asked the group, if they could go back in time, or, maybe, if a character of theirs could travel back in time, what time period would you go back to and where in the world would you be?

This gave them the opportunity of writing a short story. This time, I set the timer for twenty minutes. I suggested that they get up, stretch, walk around, make a cup of tea while they thought about what they would write, and then we could sit down and focus on the task at hand.

When we came back together again, the stories that had come out of this exercise were the makings of some great novels, or even some plays or films. One writer decided that they had been transported back to 1920s Chicago where they found themselves down a dusty alleyway with rotten cabbages, overturned trash cans and laundry hanging out to dry on lines strung between the buildings. They have given me permission to print what they wrote next:

> *I noticed a set of scuffed, patent shoes protruding from behind a dumpster at the end of the alley. A groaning sound came from the direction of the shoes.*
>
> *I edged closer to the dumpster and suddenly they saw an irate, pot-bellied man, with a dislodged trilby hat and a gash bleeding profusely from his cheek.*
>
> *"Get me up, get me up! What are you doing just standing there?" cried the man with an Italian accent.*
>
> *I reached down and helped the man up, grabbing his hat as it fell to the floor.*
>
> *The man staggered to his feet, brushed down the dirt from his suit and walked out towards the road where he hailed a cab. He insisted that I go with him, and I found myself at a seedy hotel in which it became very apparent that the man that I had saved was Al Capone.*

Another writer decided that they wanted to go back to Tudor times, to the court of Elizabeth I. They were an onlooker watching the proceedings unnoticed, something of a fly on the wall. They got to sit in on plays by Shakespeare in the Globe Theatre, to feast at the table of kings and queens, and dance with the courtiers.

I wrote a story about an old man going back to his teens. Here is what I wrote:

> *The sun was beating down on the promenade, turning the men and women in deckchairs the colour of smoked salmon. Children licked at rapidly melting ice-creams which ended up more on their noses than in their mouths. Seagulls squawked overhead, swooping down to peck at every crumb and discarded chip paper. The bells from the machines in the arcade*

on the pier competed with the whoosh and ripple of the ebb and flow of the waves on the pebbled shore.

The old man hobbled over to a bench where he sat down, picking up a discarded newspaper and cursed that he had forgotten to bring his glasses. He squinted at the headlines. Saturday, August 11, 1953. Just as he turned a page, three teenage girls came into the view. The man only had eyes for the girl in the middle with her polka-dot dress, pink headband and horn-rimmed sunglasses.

They were whispering conspiratorially as they swished passed, giggling. As the man stared at their retreating backs, the blonde in the middle stopped briefly and turned, lifting her glasses as she did so. She cocked her head to one side as she saw the old man looking at her on the bench. She smiled as he lifted his hand in greeting. In a moment they were gone into the arcade to head down to the end of the pier.

The man sat with his eyes closed, the smile ingrained on his memory, a smile of his own spreading across his pale, thin lips. He had seen her again for the first time in over ten years and it was almost as if she recognised him. He knew where she was heading with her friends, towards the café at the end of the pier, where his younger self was playing pinball and drinking Coca Cola. His heart swelled as he looked at his watch and opened his eyes, looking down the pier. Right at that moment he knew that his younger self was about to meet the love of his life and that nothing would ever be the same again.

How about you give it a go? Think about a time in history that you would like to visit, or a character that you maybe would like to write about. Where in time would it be? Where in the world would it be? What do you, or they, experience when you get there? Who do you meet? How might that experience change you or them?

I know that this exercise has for a lot of the writers in the group expanded their imaginations and got them excited about writing about different time periods. Some people are interested in writing non-fiction history or about their families through time. Others are interested in writing historical fiction, maybe embarking on some short stories or even the outline of a novel. We're getting together online for write-ins now outside of our weekly Writing for Wellness group as we start to explore the possibilities further.

What possibilities might these exercises open for you? Where might these journeys take you?

Summary

In summary, using a series of what ifs in our writing can open us up to explore a world of infinite possibilities. They can give us permission to dream dreams, think beyond our everyday lives and imagine a new kind of world that we would like to live in. These exercises can help us develop our gifts and skills, assess where we're going in life, and help us to make concrete plans.

They can also help us imagine what it is like to walk a mile in another person's shoes. As we picture a world outside of our own, we can begin to see what it is like to live in the world of another. This develops empathy and in learning to have compassion for others we also begin to have compassion for ourselves.

In the next chapter, we will look at how to build in humour and light relief in our writing, and hopefully also in our lives.

7 SOME LIGHT RELIEF

Some of the subjects that we cover in our writing for Wellness group can be a bit heavy, so I interspersed those exercises with some light relief. We literally took the time to see what is funny in our lives, what makes us smile, and what gives us the belly laugh. Through looking at these different aspects of humour, it helped us to see the funny side, both in ourselves, and in the world around us.

Activity One: Repeated Phrases

We began with a simple exercise in repeated phrases. When I was a child, we would spend our Christmas Day at my grandparents' house in Chingford, North East London. The day would go pretty much like that of other families, with the sharing of gifts, the eating of enormous meals, and the after-lunch walks in the park. We would also play party games, like the cake made of flour with a 20p coin perched precariously on the top. We would take turns to slice at the cake taking pieces off it trying to leave the coin in place. The person who sliced when the coin fell would have to go face first into the flour to retrieve it in their teeth. Much laughter was had all around.

We also recited rhymes and poetry to each other. My great-grandfather, my grandmother's father, back in the 1920s, had cut out one such rhyme from a newspaper article, stuck it on a piece of board, and would read it to his children on the night before Christmas. It was the tale of James Montgomery Farthingale. The reason I mention it here is because it had a repeated phrase in every stanza.

My grandmother learned it by heart, and at every Christmas, without fail, she would perform it for all of us. Every time we got to the line, we would shout it out together with much hilarity, "over the hearthrug and up the flue!"

We also find repeated phrases in books, plays and films. One such phrase can be found in the film Shakespeare in Love. "It's a mystery" is said repeatedly so that we smile with the familiarity of it. In the same way, in my novel that I have been writing for twelve years there is the repeated phrase of, "it's complicated." In the beginning my lead character is irritated by this phrase because she wants to know everything and understand everything about where she is. Her acceptance of it and its meaning, her ability to laugh at it and herself, is part and parcel of her journey to recovery.

For this activity I began by asking the group to think about a word or a phrase that irritated them and then I asked them to write it down. You do that now. The phrases that came up were interesting. One was, "put it away," another was, "you just have to get on with it," a third was, "because it's good for you!"

I then set the timer for 10 minutes and asked the group to write a poem, a short story, or a piece of prose using that phrase repeated over and over. There was a collective groan from the group when I asked them to do this. The last thing in the world they wanted to write about was a phrase that irritated them. But they gave it a go, nonetheless. You try it now.

When we came back together after the 10 minutes, everybody was smiling and keen to share what they had written. The person who had selected the phrase, "put it away," had written a story about a parrot who had picked up on this phrase from a drug dealer who was his former owner.

The writer who had selected, "you just have to get on with it," had written a poem about being locked in a sweet factory. "When you find yourself floating down a River of Milk Tray, you just have to get on with it! When you find yourself in a room with every flavour of gum imaginable, you just have to get on with it!"

The woman who had selected, "because it's good for you," shared with the group that she had struggled with this at first. She hadn't wanted to write anything, but she started a list beginning with writing, "you need to eat five portions of fruit and vegetables a day because it's good for you. You need to get up get, get dressed, and get out every day because it's good for you. You need to go for a walk every day because it's good for you. You need to speak to at least one person every day because it's good for you. You need to eat regular meals at regular times every day because it's good for you."

As the woman read the list out her voice changed. She began with resentment and anger, reading through gritted teeth, clearly resenting the instructions she had written. But as she started to work her way through the list, her voice cracked slightly, and a silent tear began to fall down her face. She asked for a minute to compose herself, so we moved on to somebody else until she was ready to keep going.

When she came back, she was beaming, and she asked if she could start again. This time, her tone had totally changed. She read the list as a loving mother to a cherished child. When she came to the end of the list she looked up and shared with the group how that phrase had originally come from a critical parent, and how she had rejected it because of this. This exercise had given her the opportunity to reclaim that phrase as her own and to deliver that message to herself with love and care and not judgement and criticism. She shared that she had been struggling with depression and this exercise had given her the opportunity to see what her goals needed to be in order to come out the other side. This exercise was to herself, for herself and by herself. Maybe not humorous, but certainly liberating.

Activity Two: The Ordinary in the Extraordinary

In this exercise, we looked at putting an ordinary object into an extraordinary situation. This is a technique used by many in literature and perhaps none so well as J.K. Rowling. Dumbledore's penchant for sherbet lemons, and the birthmark on his knee that was an exact replica of the London Underground map, are a case in point.

I began by asking the group to think of an ordinary object and to write it down without analysing it too much. I encouraged them to go with their first choice no matter how mundane it may have seemed. I then asked them to do some writing in which they would insert that ordinary object into an extraordinary situation. What followed were some hilarious responses. You try it now.

One writer chose an umbrella. Unlike Mary Poppins' umbrella that enabled her to fly, or the umbrellas used in the film Kingsman that enabled them to fight, this umbrella was connected to the Internet, so as they walked along the dreary, rainy streets of London, they were able to read up on the latest news, to practise their Spanish, and to select their next holiday destination.

Another writer chose a colouring book that when coloured in would enable the person to dive into the world of the coloured picture. This colouring book was a fashion-through-the-ages book, which meant, like with the exercise earlier, that they were able to travel through time and wear the clothes of the period. They're planning a visit to the Victoria and Albert Museum in London after lockdown so they can see the exhibition of costumes through the ages.

Another picked a glass tumbler which never ran dry. It was always full of water. Another picked a bed that, whenever someone got into it, would float up to the clouds so they could see the stars as they slept. One man selected a screwdriver. Can you guess he was a Doctor Who fan?

What object did you pick? Where did it take you? How did you combine the ordinary in the extraordinary? There was much laughter as we shared our writing with each other during this exercise. But it also gave us ideas. Plans were made to go on holiday, to visit museums, and even to get a light that projects stars on the ceiling of the bedroom. Why not? Anything is possible. Perhaps one day we will have umbrellas that are connected to the Internet.

Activity Three: So Funny, So Real, So True

For this exercise I asked the group to go back to their list of names and select one that they have not yet used. We spent a bit of time writing about the character, but this time I asked them to focus on their eccentricities. Did they have a funny walk? Was the tone of their voice unusual? Did they take themselves too seriously?

Charlie Chaplin was the master of the funny walk. Kenneth Williams did hilarious voices unlike anyone before or since. Hyacinth Bouquet, in the hit TV programme, "Keeping Up Appearances," was the epitome of someone who took herself too seriously and, in the process, made everybody laugh.

The reason we laugh at these funny walks, these hilarious voices and the seriousness with which some take their lives, is because we can identify with every one of those things. Who doesn't know somebody who has a funny walk? Who hasn't tried to control their laughter when listening to someone with a funny voice? Who hasn't ribbed a friend or family member for taking themselves too seriously? These things are so funny because they are so real and because they are so true.

The characters that our group wrote about were no less funny. One wrote about a boy whose hair would grow two metres every night. Another wrote about a woman who could speak in cat language. A third person wrote about a girl who skipped everywhere, another about a man you couldn't laugh, no matter how hard his family tried to make him. What does your character look like? How do they sound? Do they have a funny walk? Do they take themselves too seriously?

We then turned the lens round onto ourselves. This time I asked the group to describe themselves and their own eccentricities. Because we had warmed ourselves up by writing about a fictional character and had a good laugh sharing these descriptions with each other, it made it much easier for us to look at ourselves, our own foibles, our own peccadilloes, and the ways in which we might be taking ourselves too seriously. You try it now.

When we came back together and shared, we laughed a lot. We didn't laugh at each other, we laughed with each other, as we were able to look at ourselves in a new light and begin to be a little freer.

Activity Four: Bent All Out of Shape

Another way to look at humour is to change the size of things. Lewis Carroll in *Alice in Wonderland* had the potions to make Alice big and small. Tom Hanks in the film *Big* became an adult overnight. *The Borrowers,* Pod, Homily, and little Arrietty, were tiny people that lived below the floorboards.

The above examples are all of people changing size, and there are plenty more I could have given, but it's also funny to see objects on a different scale to their surroundings. One example of this is the giant toothbrush in the corner of Whoopi Goldberg's character's bedroom in Jumping Jack flash.

We began this exercise by thinking about what it would be like if we were big or small. We set the timer for five minutes and began to write about the world in which we were either a giant or a tiny person like the borrowers. How about you have a go now.

We really enjoyed sharing this with each other. One person wrote a story about their life as a fairy complete with delicate wings who lived in a forest with other fairies. Another wrote about living below the floorboards in a similar existence to that of the Borrowers. Only this time, a little girl lived in the house where they lived, and she had a beautiful dolls house. When she discovered the existence of the little people, she left all her dolls house furniture out with a note saying please help yourself. So, the little people who lived below the floorboards didn't have to make do with scraps and junk and instead we're able to live like kings and queens with the finest of furniture that money could buy.

Only one person wrote about being big. And it turned out that this big person felt clumsy because they kept standing on things and breaking them. Perhaps they would have preferred to have been small after all? What about you? Which did you decide to be and how did you feel about your experience?

The second part of this activity was to pick an everyday object and imagine it being either bigger or smaller than its environment. One person wrote about a giant piggy bank that came to life when the humans had gone to bed. There was an enormous pencil, a gigantic tray of chocolates, miniature books that lined the walls of a great library for ants and delicate, microscopic sewing kits use by microscopic people that live inside our bodies, sewing it back together when it becomes damaged. What about you? What object did you pick and was it big or small?

Activity Five: We Know Something They Don't Know

A classic use of humour is to give the reader or the audience some information that a key character doesn't know. For those of you who have never been to an English pantomime, I highly recommend you investigate it. This interactive children's romp through a fairy tale is laced with jokes that will be understood by different generations in different ways and at different times, making it the perfect family outing around Christmas.

One line, unscripted because it nearly always comes from the children in the audience is, "he's behind you." The lovable character who is front centre stage is asking the children if they know where the villain is, seemingly oblivious to the fact that they are literally behind them. The children scream this out to the character who just doesn't seem to get it. Children love this kind of humour.

For the purposes of this exercise, I had the group write a conversation between two people, real or imagined, one of whom knew something that the other did not. One writer wrote a telephone conversation between two people in which the first was passing along some major gossip to the second. We laughed out loud at this, probably because we have all been caught doing the same thing ourselves at some point or can certainly relate in some way.

Another scene was one in which a parent refused to tell a child what presents they had been bought for Christmas. The scavenger hunt which followed as the child tried to find the secret hiding place of said gifts around the house was hilarious.

A third, was not funny at all, but we always say let the pen lead your words and go wherever it may take you. This was a conversation between a doctor and a patient in which the doctor had to give the bad news about a loved one. Drawing on painful personal experiences like this can be incredibly cathartic when using fictional characters as it creates a safe space in which we can allow ourselves to feel. And feel we did. There wasn't a dry eye in the meeting. One thing we did learn in all of this is that there is a very fine line between comedy and tragedy.

Activity Six: Out of Place

Like the, "ordinary in the extraordinary," activity, putting something or someone out of place can also provide some light relief and potentially create humour. A stiff upper lipped Englishman with OCD, starched shirts and a full suit arriving to work as a policeman on a Caribbean island is a case in point. The television programme, *Death in Paradise*, uses the concept of an out of place person to generate humour.

The random boot lying on the grass at the top of a hill that is a portkey in Harry Potter is another case in point, as are masses of owls in a suburban street in Surrey. The grotesque fish in the basket on the boat in Mama Mia was hilarious. Even a flower growing up through the cracks of a pavement in downtown New York can provoke a smile.

I had the group think about what kind of object might appear out of place in a different setting. We had camels in Cambridge, inflatable vegetables in a swimming pool, people walking on water, chocolate rain and a woman who lived in a well. Have a go yourself and let me know how you get on.

Summary

It's always good when embarking on a Writing for Wellness journey to include times of light relief, laughter and humour. There are various ways to do this, whether it be by repeating a phrase, inserting the ordinary in the extraordinary, writing caricatures of a person's eccentricities, changing the size of something, having one person know something that another does not, or simply putting something in the wrong place.

Light and shade are a natural part of our journey in life. We cannot live forever on the top of a mountain, no matter how ecstatic we might feel up there and how beautiful the views may be. But we do need those mountain-top experiences in our lives that will fuel us for the parts of the journey when we are in the valleys. Nothing grows on the mountain top, but there is the potential for rich vegetation in the valleys. So too for us in our own lives.

Yet even if we set out for a mountain-top experience, a touch of humour, or a bit of light relief, we never know where the pen is going to take us. Sometimes, what we hoped would be funny, ends up being excruciating. Equally, what starts out serious can end up being funny. The important thing is to keep putting one foot in front of the other and to enjoy the journey, knowing that the further along we go the greater freedom we will find.

In the next chapter, we will examine what it means to focus on the positive things in our lives.

8 THE HALF-FULL GLASS

During lockdown, surrounded by the threat of coronavirus, it's very easy to focus on the negative things in life and to catastrophize. That's not to say that we shouldn't keep it real, and recognise that there is a time for tears, a time to grieve, a time for sorrow. But in my experience, when we also allow time to explore the good in ourselves and in each other, to count our blessings so to speak, this can lift our mood and help us to face a brighter tomorrow.

Over the weeks that we have met as a group I have incorporated several exercises that helped us to think about this in different ways. I'll share some of those exercises with you here.

Activity One: Gratitude List

The first activity was very simple. I asked the group to think about 10 things that they were grateful for. How about you have a go at that now. Here is the list that I made:

God
Family
Friends
My home
My cat, Henry
Technology
Writing
Crafts
Music
Nature

Are any of the things that are on my list also on yours? When we got back together as a group and shared our lists with each other we had some duplicates, but we were also able to start to see some of the things which were uniquely important to us. Those of us who have a faith put God on our list. Not everybody has a pet, but those that do included their pet on their list. Some people said technology, but others spoke in general terms about the meetings that they had been able to attend online such as their knit and natter group. Not only did this exercise give us the opportunity to appreciate the things that we value most in our lives, it also helped us to learn a fair amount about each other.

Pretty much all the people in the group, including myself, felt that we could have written more given half the chance. The more we wrote about our gratitudes, the more gratitudes we wanted to write about. Several of the people in the group decided that they would incorporate a gratitudes list into their daily journals. We always speak about how our journalling is going at the start of every meeting and these people fed back to us that writing a daily gratitudes list was improving their mood during lockdown.

Activity Two: 100 Things I Love/Like

This next activity took a little longer. I asked the group to write 100 things that they liked or loved. I gave them plenty of time and space to think about these things. Some went for a short walk around their gardens, others closed their eyes in order to meditate, others still went and made a cup of tea. Many of them just started writing, without thinking too much about it.

Not everybody made it to 100, but a lot of them did, especially the ones who listed each person that they cared about individually. The ones who simply said family or friends struggled a bit. One lady took quite up quite a chunk of her writing listing all the food that she enjoys and then moved on to talk about chocolate bars. Another, an animal lover, listed all the animals that she loves. The important thing about all these exercises is that there are no right or wrong answers. All this writing is to you, for you and by you.

How about you have a go and see if you can write 100 things that you either like or love? Did you manage to reach 100? Did you struggle? How did you feel after you had written the list? Did it make you want to do some of the things that you love more? Did it make you want to reach out to some of the people that you love? When we talked amongst ourselves in the group about how we felt about what we had done a few people said that this kind of list, although difficult to write at times, was a useful tool in helping them to prioritise their lives.

Activity Three: Mirror, Mirror, On the Wall

This activity was difficult for a lot of people, and even painful for some. I got the members of the group to fetch a mirror and to use it to look at themselves and write ten things that they liked about themselves. As we sat there writing a few them groaned that they couldn't do it and didn't want to do it. One important thing about this group is that I never make anybody do anything that they don't want to do. One person decided to opt out and that was fine. If you come across any of the activities in this book and feel that you don't want to do them that doesn't mean you're not working through this journey properly. One of the biggest things that I always say is take what you need and leave the rest behind.

If you feel up to it, fetch a mirror, and have a go at this exercise. If you don't, that's fine. Just skip this activity and move on to the next one. Those that wanted to in our group persevered and ended up writing at least a few things that they liked about themselves. These could be physical attributes, personality traits, or even levels of intelligence. Again, as with all things that we write about, there are no limits.

If you did take part in this exercise, how did you feel about it? Did you struggle to write your list? Are there parts of yourself that you would prefer not to focus on? Another activity that we did later was to take some of those parts that we didn't like and give them to a fictional character. This character was a vulnerable character, a sympathetic character, and then we would insert ourselves into the story and speak to this character about those traits or features with love. Perhaps you might like to try and do the same with yours.

One lady was full of gratitude for the ability to write this list with acceptance that she was who she was. She had spent the greater part of her life wishing she was somebody else, wanting to look different, wanting to sound different, and trying to act differently in order to please others and to meet an invisible standard that was inside her head. As she has gone along on her own Writing for Wellness journey, she has found a way to nurture herself, to cherish herself and to accept herself as being exactly the way she is supposed to be today.

Activity Four: A Force for Good

In another week, we spent some time looking at a person, place, thing, or situation which has had a positive impact on our lives. We set the timer for 10 minutes, and just started writing. I struggled to do this exercise, not because I couldn't think of what to write about, but because I had too many choices and I wanted to write about all of them! I decided to settle for the first thing that came into my head – Mothecombe Beach.

Mothecombe Beach is part of the Fleet Estate on the South Devon coast. It is perhaps best known as the backdrop for a very famous scene in the film Sense and Sensibility starring Kate Winslet. Her character is caught in the rain when she twists her ankle in a field and is then rescued by the seemingly dashing Willoughby. That field overlooks the beach. Yet my relationship with that beach goes back to my early childhood, way before that film was ever imagined. Here is what I wrote:

I was five, and we were on holiday in South Devon again. It was a beautiful summer's day, and there wasn't a cloud in the sky, as we pulled into the field to park the car next to the old school that had always been a cafe to me, and the source of ice cream.

I climbed gingerly out of the back seat as my siblings ran on ahead of me. "Wait for me!" I cried. But they were already gone, clambering down the narrow, steep path interspersed with boulders and stones and canopied with arching, gnarled trees. I had to move slowly, for my arm was in a sling, having broken my collar bone just a short time before.

I wasn't alone, my dad was right in front of me, picnic hamper in one hand, and a cricket bat, buckets and spades, and a set of boules in the other. He had a camera on a strap around his neck. Behind me was my mum, carrying the towels, a blanket, sun scream and changes of clothes. "Careful!" she kept saying to me, as she anxiously watched my progress.

Once on the beach, I sat in my bikini on a towel, trying to dig with my left hand, getting frustrated as I did so. The others played near the water's edge while my dad went back to the car to fetch the dingy and the pump.

Once the dingy was inflated, a discussion ensued between my parents about whether I would be allowed to go on the water. My dad won, and I was allowed in. It felt so good to be out on the sea, bobbling around in that cove that day. We could see my mum waving at us from the beach as she sat there, leaning against a rock, reading a magazine.

Back on shore, we lit a fire and cooked sausages on forks which we ate between floury baps. We then played games, but I didn't do very well with my wrong hand, and soon grew weary of it.

As the sun start to grow low over the fields, we packed up our things and made our way up to the hill to the car. The café was still open, so we went inside and had ice-creams from a lovely lady who let us choose our own while my parents sipped on cups of tea and ate sticky buns.

Thirty years later, my mum and I took the same trip to Mothecombe Beach. There were no more fires on the sand, nor dinghies in the water. My arms were free, but my legs were weary. I took even longer getting down that hill, even though the path was decidedly shorter than I had remembered.

After we spent some time, paddling in the surf, we dried the sand from between our toes and made our way back up to the café in the field. As we went in, and ordered our teas and a sticky bun, I felt the familiar warmth come from the lady behind the counter, and I told her that I used to come here as a child.

"You're the girl with her arm in a sling," she said. "I'd recognise that beautiful smile anywhere."

That same woman had been working in that café every summer for over thirty years and she remembered me. I will never forget her and her kindness and friendliness to me, both as a child when my arm was in a sling and as an adult, when the pain in my legs was almost more than I could bear.

OK, so that's not quite what I expected to write about. Others ended up going off on tangents too. One person wrote about their favourite teacher, another about the teddy bear they had as a child. I could have written about the retired missionary who lived across the street from me as a teen who I would visit with and sit by her three-bar fire in the height of summer, drinking tea and eating stale biscuits whilst listening to her fantastic tales of her adventures around the world.

One person wrote about the time they were invited to a garden party at Buckingham Palace. Now you know my bucket list, you can imagine how jealous I was to hear about that! Another wrote a powerful piece about the time they were drowning in Lyme Regis bay when they were rescued a man in a dinghy. The list is endless, and the possibilities are infinite.

Activity Five: I Feel Amazing When...

This activity involved another writing prompt where we simply wrote out the line, "I feel amazing when..." and kept writing. How about you have a go at doing that now?

We'd covered the things that we're grateful for, the things that we love or like, the positive things that we think about ourselves, and the forces for good in the world around us. Now, we gave ourselves the opportunity to think about the different things that we could do that would make us feel amazing. Here is what I wrote:

I feel amazing when I've had a good night's sleep and I wake in the morning feeling refreshed and rejuvenated. I feel amazing when I have a day where I have energy and I'm pain free. I feel amazing when the sun shines and I can feel its rays gently caressing my cheeks. I feel amazing when I get the opportunity to go for a walk-through nature, to hear the bird sing, to see the flowers bloom, and to hear the wind rustling through the trees.

I feel amazing when I go sailing and can feel the wind in my hair and can lean out over the side of a boat as the sail is close hauled, and I'm beating my instructors by stealing their wind in a race. I feel amazing when I get to ride a horse that I can communicate with and be in tune with. I feel amazing when I'm on that horse in the middle of the Isle of Skye, with no one else around me, as a lamb pokes his head out from behind the legs of his mother. As I begin to canter, he skips alongside me.

I feel amazing when I worship God, when I'm lifted to his throne, when I sing his praises with song, and when I feel filled with his spirit. I felt amazing when I read something that inspires me, when I brainstorm with other creative people, and when I write something new. I feel amazing when I finish a craft project, when I gather people together in community with each other, when I see them come alive and thrive. I feel amazing when I see somebody who is afraid or has doubts about themselves step out into their own, discover their gifts and their skills, and become empowered to use them in the world.

I feel amazing when I play ABBA and dance and sing and twirl like I did as a child. I feel amazing when I see family that I haven't seen in a long time, when I get to visit new and exciting places, share a precious meal with friends, or spend some time tickling my cat under his chin. I feel amazing when I take the time to stop and remember that I am truly alive.

I wish I could print everybody's contributions here. They were all amazing. People talked about holding their babies in their arms for the first time. They shared what it felt like to receive an award for their work, to be the first person in their family to graduate from university, and to be able to make a recipe that was as good as their grandmother's. The life force that flowed through this writing was completely inspirational and certainly energised us for the rest of the meeting, if not the day.

How did you feel about this experience? Did it energise and inspire you? I'd love to hear from you and to hear about what makes you feel amazing.

Activity Six: Tomorrow's World

In this exercise I asked the group to imagine the future. Some found this really difficult because they have a lot of fear about what lies ahead.

One lady is a member of a local gym where there is a swimming pool. She has found that her mental health is radically improved when she is able to go swimming regularly. She hasn't been able to do this for the last couple of months and this has really affected her. She has found it difficult to find any semblance of a routine in her life. For her, the jokes about having a daytime set of pyjamas and a night-time set of pyjamas during lockdown are all too real. She has struggled to plan her meals ahead of time and to eat at regular times. Motivating herself to do anything at all, including leaving the house to go for a walk, has been as difficult as wading through treacle. She really misses her regular swims.

However, she is terrified of going back out there again. It's not the pool that she is afraid of; after all, there's probably enough chlorine in there to kill any virus. She's afraid of the changing rooms. When she took part in this exercise she talked about a time in the future when she would no longer be afraid to go out of her front door. She talked about a time in the future when there would be a vaccine for this virus and the fear that so many of us have carried around during this time would fade into our distant memories. She also talked about a time when she could swim again, when she could breathe again without worrying about what germs she might pick up along the way.

Another writer decided to approach this exercise as if they were writing an episode of Tomorrow's World. In it they imagined all sorts of new gadgets and breakthroughs in science that might happen soon. I think this is quite difficult to do nowadays, particularly because there have been so many rapid technological advances in recent years. But he certainly came up with some interesting ones. There was the chip that you could insert in your ear every time you wanted to speak a new language, there were the floating cars that were propelled by recycled cardboard from Amazon deliveries. There were the machines that could produce a three course meal at the touch of a button. He even had the ideal Mars home exhibition in which people could sample various biospheres in which to live on Mars.

What might the future look like for you? What are you looking forward to? What might you do today that will lead towards a different tomorrow?

Summary

In this chapter we have spent some time focusing on the half full glass in our lives. It is all too easy when surrounded by the unprecedented situation in which we find ourselves to focus on the negative and fail to see the silver lining behind the dark cloud. We began focusing on the things that we're grateful for, we spent a concerted amount of time thinking about the things that we love or like, we faced ourselves in the mirror and challenged ourselves to find something that is good looking back at us. We also spent some time thinking about the people, places, things and situations in our lives that have been a force for good.

Sometimes we have discovered the positive forces that have been at work in our lives, even, and sometimes especially, during adversity. We have taken happy trips down memory lanes to the experiences in our lives that have brought us joy. We have spent time refilling our tanks by writing about the things that make us feel amazing and experiencing the buzz we get by sharing those things with each other. We have looked to the future and thought about the things that we're looking forward to and what we can do today to help us with tomorrow.

In our next chapter we will be looking at the different ways in which visual prompts, in the form of postcards, photographs, and other images, might help us in our Writing for Wellness journey.

9 VISUAL PROMPTS

When beginning writing, the first sense that people tend to focus on is sight. It is often so much easier for us to describe what we see than it is for us to talk about what we hear, taste, touch or can smell. Visual prompts are still an incredible tool to use in order to unlock our imaginations, stir our memories, and assist us on our Writing for Wellness journeys.

There are a multitude of different visual images that we can use, and I have used several of them in exercises throughout the weeks that the group has been meeting. Below are samples of the types of visual prompts we have looked at and the kinds of writing and responses to writing that came out of them.

Activity One: Postcards

For this first exercise I asked the group to bring with them to the meeting a postcard of one of their favourite places or things. We had everything from the grand canal in Venice to the Houses of Parliament in London. One person even brought a postcard that was a photograph of their great uncle who fought in the First World War.

We spent some time describing what we saw in the postcard. How about you do it now? Find a postcard that is meaningful to you and spend some time writing about it. As with the other exercises, don't be afraid to go off on tangents. If the image conjures up memories, thoughts or feelings that go beyond the boundaries of the card, just go with it and see where it takes you.

The card I selected depicts scenes from Devon, which, when you remember my description of Mothecombe Beach, is perhaps not surprising. It has never been written on, and is in pristine condition, so I must have picked it up on one of my trips to Devon over the years.

I suppose you could say that I was cheating as my card has four different pictures on it, but I chose to focus on the family of Dartmoor ponies in the top left corner. This exercise reminded me how much I love to be in Devon, how I long to be out in nature, and how I absolutely adore horses. You might also remember that horses featured quite heavily on my bucket list. Perhaps Father Christmas will be kind to me one day and I'll get to own one, but in the meantime, I am content to look at this postcard and imagine. This exercise also reminded me that I once adopted a horse called Oops a Daisy on the Outer Banks of North Carolina, but that's a whole other story. Here is what I wrote:

> *Were it not for the sun beating down on the gorse bushes, this blustery day would have come cold to these new-borns. The chestnut mare preens the one, while the other snuggles up in the grass for a much-needed rest. Once the wash is over, they will be able to scamper free, drink from the cool river that ripples and gurgles over pebbles and stones. They will be able to canter with their friends and even practise jumping over small bushes. Then, as the sun begins to set, and the shadows form in the valleys, they will re-join the herd while they munch on some grass and their father tells them tales of the ponies long ago.*

For many in the group this exercise was simply a pleasant diversion during lockdown. With all the negative visual images in the news, it was a refreshing relief to be able to focus on something beautiful and evocative.

For some however, as they allowed the words to flow, and wrote beyond the edges of the pictures, this exercise brought up unexpected emotions of experiences that they had enjoyed as children and had not allowed themselves to do again, of places they had been to with loved ones lost, and the family members they had never met but somehow when writing about had felt a greater connection to than they had ever felt before.

Visual images can be incredibly powerful and evocative. The only problem is that with the advent of the smartphone and the worldwide web we are bombarded with images every day. It's all too easy to experience sensory overload and when this happens the brain just simply begins to shut down.

In Writing for Wellness and using visual prompts we discovered the importance of looking up from our screens and out at the views around us. We also began to realise the ways in which our intake of images can have a profound effect on our mental health. Many of us made a conscious decision to just stop looking at the news all day every day and instead to either read it or listen to it once a day.

When we began to do this our heads began to clear, we started to notice the beautiful things around us more, our moods lifted, and we found ourselves much more present in the moment and with others.

Activity Two: The Country Walk

This next activity involved some more homework. I asked the group when they were on their daily walk to take photographs using their phones. They then brought these photographs with them to the next meeting and we spent some time writing descriptions of our favourite ones.

Some had taken close-ups of flowers or gnarled pieces of bark, others of stunning views of fields and woods. Some had taken selfies with their walks in the background. What they all said was that walking with the intention of taking photographs made them pay closer attention to their environment as they thought about composition and light and how to capture a moment. One lady even made a video so that she could record the birdsong.

Perhaps you might like to try taking photographs when you next go for a walk. It doesn't have to be a country walk. We are fortunate here in this corner of Hertfordshire to be very close to open fields, parkland and woods, but an urban or suburban setting can be equally inspiring and beautiful. Take lots of photos and pick your favourite.

The people who had taken selfies chose not to use those images to write about. There is something so raw and revealing when challenged with writing about our contemporary selves. It is difficult enough to write about our younger selves, let alone the self we see in the mirror today.

Just as with the postcard exercise, the photos of flowers and of pretty views were a welcome distraction during life in lockdown. But it was more than a pretty view. It was an appreciation for the beauty that is around us and with that came gratitude for what we have on our doorsteps.

That is one thing which has increased during this frightening time, gratitude. As we chatted and shared in the group over the weeks, we came to realise how much we had taken for granted in our lives. As we wrote about these scenes on our daily walks, we started to appreciate just how much we had and to count our blessings so to speak. It is our sincere hope that we will not lose that attitude of gratitude when all of this is past, and we go back to whatever semblance of normality this virus will permit.

Activity Three: Abandoned Places

I've always enjoyed this visual prompt. I've been on several writing retreats and courses over the years and on one such course we did a postcard prompt where we got to choose from a few cards that the instructor had brought in. I selected the postcard of a derelict castle. As I sat there looking at the image, I didn't see a lifeless pile of stones, what I saw was the castle coming to life, the mud and straw on the floor by the stables, the blacksmith hammering on a sword, knights riding off into battle, and the sheriff feasting and drinking with his family.

Using images of abandoned places as visual prompts tests the imagination to the full. I selected a series of abandoned places and put them into a collage which I shared with the group. I asked them to pick one of the images and to write about what they saw. Not every abandoned building had to be rebuilt in their minds and on the pages. I simply asked that they begin writing about what they saw and then allowed their minds to wander and see where the pen took them.

There were six images in all. After much searching, I found the picture of the abandoned castle that I had used before. There was an abandoned warehouse in Birmingham, a derelict house made of grey stone in the middle of the Yorkshire Moors, and a gutted church. There was also an old red abandoned barn somewhere in America, and a house in London, one side of which was blown away in the Blitz.

Do a search for abandoned buildings online and have a go at this yourself. Try finding a selection of different types of buildings in different locations. One image I nearly used was an old fairground where the plants and trees had pushed their way up through the pavement and were beginning to ensnare the rollercoaster. I found it decidedly unsettling, which is perhaps why I veered away from it, but maybe I should have kept it in precisely because of the emotional reactions it evoked in me.

Some of the group took this exercise literally and described precisely what they saw in the image. Others rebuilt the buildings in their minds and imagined what life would have been like inside when the lights were on. Others kept on writing until, in their imaginations, they began to picture an entire world where this building existed. As a result of this, there has been an increased desire from some to write historical fiction and others discovered a new time period that they are interested in reading about.

Others looked at these images from a metaphorical perspective. As they wrote about the empty buildings, they explored the sometimes-hollow feelings inside each of us. They talked about their emotions, how the piles of rubble made them feel, and as they wrote they began to reconnect with parts of themselves that had been lost or neglected. This exercise made them want to rebuild aspects of their lives that had become derelict or unused.

Life in lockdown has given us plenty of opportunities to stop and reflect about the direction in which we are going. Many in our group have discovered that we much prefer to work from home and to spend more time with our families then to spend countless hours commuting back and forth to fluorescent-lit offices in polluted cities.

Others have surprised themselves with how much they have enjoyed home schooling their children, coming up with interactive and inventive lessons. Some have even explored the possibility of continuing to home school their children after lockdown and have formed groups with other like-minded parents so that they can potentially pool their resources.

For many, it has simply been a question of endurance. Whether they live alone or with others, this entire experience has put an enormous strain on their mental health. Whether working from home, teaching their children, living alone or with family, or being a frontline worker, life in lockdown has been a living hell. In order to survive we have all had to learn to ask for help, to reach out to others, and to share how we are feeling. In order to survive we have had to adapt very quickly to what has become a new normal. One of the multitude of ways in which our group has survived has been to come together once a week and to write it out, one word at a time.

Activity Four: Landscapes

Once again, I put together a collage for this exercise. This collage contained a series of images of different types of landscapes. The first was a lunar landscape, an image taken of the surface of the moon with its craters, rocks and dust. The second was a desert landscape with its undulating ripples of mountainous sand leading off into an impenetrable distance while the sun beat down relentlessly from a cloudless sky.

The third was a seascape with foamy waves crashing against sheer cliffs as dark clouds loomed overhead. The fourth was an Alpine scene that would have fitted into the pages of Heidi, complete with chalets and picture postcard snow-capped mountains. Then there was a Tuscan scene. I couldn't very well do this without an image of my beloved Italy. The cypress trees pointed upwards from the edges of distant fields while the morning dew glistened on the leaves and ripened fruit in a nearby vineyard.

The last image was a city skyline, New York City to be precise. I had bought this postcard in 2002 on a trip to New York with my aunt to see my great uncle who lived there. It had been a wonderful visit spent in marvellous company and we even got to see a production of thoroughly modern Millie on Broadway. We still think he was in the CIA by the way, but that is a whole series of stories for another day.

On the last day I had some extra time and felt a strong urge to visit Ground Zero. When I emerged from the subway I was overwhelmed by a deep sense of sorrow. The entire site was surrounded by a chain link fence and they were still clearing the debris from the middle. To one side of the plaza was a church with a graveyard in the front and all the stones we're leaning away from the middle. The sides facing the Plaza were black with soot. The other sides were cleaner. People had threaded flowers into the chain link fence and everywhere around the outside people stood in silence. There were no words.

The card I had brought back from New York was of its skyline at night. Until I had gone to pay for it, I hadn't realised that it was an old card and the twin towers were still there. This image prompted several people to write about 9/11. Everybody remembers where they were that day but not everybody has had a chance to write about it and for those people, perhaps for the first time, it gave them a chance to express their grief at the enormous loss of life that September morning.

Activity Five: Portraits

This activity is a great way to think about characters again. Once more I did a series of six pictures put together into a collage. There was a Masai warrior, an old woman in India with a face so lined every moment of her life seemed carved out in her cheeks. There was a young Chinese woman in beautiful red and gold silk celebrating the Chinese New Year, a businessman in a pin striped suit, bowler hat and glasses, and a little girl living on the rubbish dumps in the border towns of Mexico. The last image was a face of a woman with no background, no context, just a face full of fear.

During this time of lockdown there's been an interesting programme on the BBC called "The Great British Intelligence Test." At least a quarter of a million people across the UK have taken part in an online test which examines different aspects of a person's intelligence, everything from emotional intelligence to spatial awareness. One part of the test looked at our ability to read micro expressions. These are the emotions that are displayed fleetingly on our faces by way of reflex before we have time to compose ourselves.

One television programme to come out of America was "Lie to Me" starring Tim Roth. He played a man who had an uncanny ability to read peoples micro expressions and as a result was able to deduce whether a person was telling the truth. I think that there is a direct correlation between our ability to read these expressions on the faces of others and our ability to empathise with them.

This exercise gave us the opportunity to take a moment to explore the expressions on the face of another human being, to read what was in their eyes, to imagine what their lives were like, and to walk a mile in their shoes. It also gave us the opportunity to explore our own feelings, to think about our own micro expressions, to write about our fears, our anger, our frustrations, our guilt and shame.

It also gave us the chance to be creative, to embellish the lives of the characters that we saw in the pictures and try to imagine what their name might be, where they lived, what they did, how they thought. By using pictures from around the globe it gave us the opportunity to think about life beyond our own borders and to embrace the humanity in us all. Why don't you have a go for yourself? Do share with me how you got on.

Activity Six: Pathways

Another visual prompt we used was a series of pictures of pathways. The first was a flagstone pathway weaving its way across a neatly manicured lawn, surrounded by borders of flowers. The pathway lead to a humpback bridge which went over a small creek. This was a garden pathway. The second image was of a pathway made of wooden slats, weathered by the salty air, which led to an island in the middle of a turquoise sea. The island itself was full of dense vegetation covered in deciduous trees and palms. The third was a dusty track strewn with twigs and pebbles which wound its way through a dense pine forest. At the base of the trees was thick foliage of bracken and ferns. The final pathway was more of a tunnel which led under enormous tanks filled with fish and other marine wildlife. Clearly a pathway found in an aquarium.

I asked the group to select one of these images and then to write about it. I asked them to think about where the path had come from and where it might be going to, who might walk on that path, and what the sights, sounds, smells etc. were along the path. As with all these writing exercises, I reminded the group that if they felt themselves going off piste, or in this case off path, just to go with the flow and see where the pen took them.

One of the exciting things about simply creating a space in which people can write and throwing into the mix a series of different types of writing prompts, is that you never know where they're going to land. The people in my group always joke that I am never satisfied until somebody in the group has cried each week. Obviously, I don't set out with the intention of reducing someone to tears, I simply create space, a safe space, in which people can share where they know that they will be loved, accepted, and encouraged.

Watching the members of the group develop trust for each other and for the writing process over the course of the weeks was nothing short of a privilege. The way I like to describe it is that it's like watching the flowers bloom as people are liberated from their fears and empowered to pursue their dreams. I know the book won't come close to generating that same experience for you, but I am listening and if you want to share your writing with me don't forget to use the hash tag #writingforwellness. Equally, don't be afraid to use this book as inspiration for starting your own Writing for Wellness group wherever you may be. Even if you live a million miles away from anyone, providing you have access to the Internet, there is absolutely no reason in the world why you can't start a group as well.

I always have a lot of fun putting the images together for the visual writing prompts. I use shutterstock.com for the images and canva.com to put them together. Perhaps you might like to have a go at putting together some visual prompts of your own. The themes are unlimited, and you can be as creative with them as you are with your own writing. In addition to pathways we also did a writing prompt one week of a garden shed producing some hilarious responses from the group. What theme would you choose for a visual prompt? Have a go at putting it together, choose one of the images to write about, and just write.

Summary

Sight is often the first sense that we experience in a new place. It is the easiest sense to describe. Using a variety of visual prompts, it is possible to unlock the imagination, stir up memories, and process our emotions.

There are an infinite number of different types of visual writing prompts that we can use. Some, like postcards, are given to us. Others are images that we capture for ourselves whether they be of our own artistic creation or photographs that we take on our daily walks. Others still are sourced online or elsewhere.

No matter where they come from, they can still act as powerful tools to facilitate our Writing for Wellness. The magical thing about creating a space in which to write, and then using a series of prompts to get us started, is that we never know where it will land, what it will provoke in us, and how it might set us free.

In our next chapter we will be looking at the source of inspiration and asking ourselves who and what inspires us.

10 INSPIRATION

As I said earlier on in the book, I have always been fascinated with the question of where inspiration and imagination come from. In this chapter, we will look at the people places, things and situations that have inspired us in our lives and create some space and some prompts that I hope will inspire us further.

I have been very fortunate to have been surrounded by creative people for most of my life. Whether they be writers, readers, artists, musicians, crafters or other expansive thinkers, I have found myself inspired by them all. These people have been trailblazers and guiding lights in my life, they have opened my world to new ideas, new ways of thinking, and dreams, and have encouraged me to follow my aspirations.

The words inspiration and aspiration come from the Latin verb spirare which means to breathe. When we are inspired, we are breathing in and when we aspire to do something we're breathing out. There is a Hebrew word, ruah, which means the spirit, wind or breath of God. When we are inspired, we breathe in God's spirit. When we aspire, we seek to share God spirit with the world. We are holistic beings made up of a body, a mind and a spirit. When we reconcile to this fact, we open ourselves up to creativity and inspiration and in turn aspire to share that creativity and inspiration with others. When we do this, we experience what it truly means to be alive.

Activity One: Favourite Teacher

We began by looking at our favourite teacher. I asked the group to describe their favourite teacher and to talk about what made them so special. I got them to think about the different ways these teachers had inspired them in their lives and to what extent that inspiration lasted to this day. You have a go at doing that now.

Here is what I wrote:

My favourite teacher was Mrs Ridgeley. I was lucky to have her for two years at the end of my time in junior school after having endured a previously difficult year. Mrs Ridgeley was tall and poised with short white hair and pink lipstick. She would wear pencil skirts and short heels and was the epitome of a trendy woman from the 1980s.

She was also the mother of Andrew Ridgeley of Wham fame, and the band became famous during that two-year period. I will always remember her coming into the classroom one day buzzing with excitement. It was a Thursday and she told all of us that her son was in a band and they were going to be on Top of the Pops that evening. In those days, Top of the Pops was filmed on a Thursday and broadcast on a Friday evening. She explained to us that another band had dropped out at the last minute and that Wham had been asked to take their place. George and Andrew, Pepsi and Shirley, made up a very quick dance routine, threw on some white tee shirts, and danced their way into the charts as they sang Young Guns.

I decided that it would be nice if they came to our school for our Christmas party and so I wrote them a letter of invitation and got the whole school to sign it. I left it on Mrs Ridgeley's desk and a few days later a reply appeared pinned to the pegboard in the classroom in which they had accepted the invitation! Andrew judged a dancing competition and he and Shirley sat at my table while we ate chocolate cake and crisps.

But despite the excitement of being a witness to the rise of stars, what I really liked about Mrs Ridgeley was that she saw potential in me. There were times when I struggled, not academically, but emotionally. The experiences of the previous year had taken their toll on me and I had become extremely sensitive and at times fragile. But Mrs Ridgeley never gave up on me, always invested in me, and had the amazing capacity of making everybody in the class feel special, no matter what their academic progress, sporting ability, or artistic talent might be.

She was also an incredibly creative teacher, devising lessons that I remember to this day. There was the session about the differences between similes and metaphors, the help she gave in showing us the political bias of various newspapers and radio broadcasts, the writing activities that she set for us after we watched the television programme, "How We Used to Live," and the trust that she placed in me when I announced that I would like to write a biography of Al Capone when I was just 11 years old.

She also encouraged my creative writing. I still have the exercise books with the notes that she wrote in the margins. At the end of one, she wrote the words that have stuck with me ever since, "If you apply yourself and work really hard at it, one day I believe that you will become a wonderful writer." I hope she would be proud of what I am doing here today.

As we shared our stories amongst the group of the inspirational men and women who had taught us, we were deeply moved by what we heard. One story has stayed with me. It is Haley's story. She had so many inspirational teachers that she went on to become a teacher herself and I know for a fact that she is inspiring countless generations to come. The inspiration she received and breathed in she has turned around into aspiration to be shared with others.

Activity Two: Favourite Author

As you will know from my bucket list, I am a bit of a fan of J.K. Rowling. When somebody creates something new and ground-breaking, a multitude of people try to replicate what that person has done. The number of books about magic that came out in the wake of the Harry Potter series is a case in point. I don't find J.K. Rowling inspirational because I want to be her. I don't want to create another Harry Potter series. I find J.K. Rowling inspirational because she has an unfettered imagination, and a natural ability to tell stories. She has succeeded in creating an entire fictional world from her own imagination which she has then invited the rest of the world to participate in. The best inspiration comes from people that we admire, not because we want to be them, but because they show us what it is like to become a realisation of our creative selves.

I began this exercise by asking the group to put the name of their favourite author at the top of the page. I then got them to spend a bit of time writing about what they love about that author and why they enjoy reading their books. Finally, I asked them how these authors inspired them in their own writing, not to replicate them, but as a launchpad for something new.

For example, one lady talked about her love of Beatrix Potter. She is a friend to animals anyway, and as a child took great delight in reading the stories about Jemima Puddleduck, Jeremy Fisher and Squirrel Nutkin. She delights in the way Beatrix Potter brought her animals to life, giving them relatable, human qualities.

Another member of the group wrote about Stephen King. They're not a fan of horror films, saying that they have ample imagination of their own without needing to be scared by someone else, but they are a huge fan of Stephen King's other work, especially their favourite film, the Shawshank Redemption. What they like about Stephen King beyond being a fan of this novel, is his tenacity of spirit and his work ethic. Stephen King is one of the most prolific writers in the English language today, because he writes consistently, even when he doesn't feel like it, and this really inspired the member of the group to set aside time on a regular basis to write.

When I did this exercise on another occasion, I wrote about Charlotte

Bronte. I read Jane Eyre for the first time when I was 13 years old on a holiday in Greece. I became an immediate fan and went on to read the book several times throughout my education. I even wrote my undergraduate dissertation on the struggle between passion and duty in the life and novels of Charlotte Bronte. I spent a very pleasant summer staying at a bed and breakfast in Haworth, Yorkshire, walking up the cobbled street every morning, past the pub where Branwell drank, and through the graveyard to the parsonage. I would sit in the library in the new wing and began reading everything that Charlotte had ever written. I then went on to read everything that had ever been written about Charlotte and her writing. But I needed more, and as I sat looking out of the library window it dawned on me, I needed to get inside her head, and the best way to do that was to read what she read.

I asked the librarian to give me a list of all the books that were known to have been owned by Charlotte in particular. As I scanned down that list, I came across the title by Isaac Watts, clergyman and hymn writer. The paraphrased title of this book was "Passions and How to Control Them." I became rather passionate myself and could hardly contain my excitement. I asked the librarian if I could see the book. She explained to me that because of its value and rarity I would need to get special permission from my professor at university. Unfortunately, he was on a lecture tour of Canada at the time and completely unreachable. Dejected, I went back to my digs at the bed and breakfast.

Over breakfast the next morning, I fell into a conversation with a lady from Maryland who, as it turned out, was a professor at the University of Maryland who was in the UK filming a documentary on the Brontes. When I explained my situation to her, she offered to vouch for me and sign the paperwork that would enable me to get access to the book. On a Wednesday morning, with hands shaking, wearing gloves and using a pencil, I gingerly opened to the front page, and there in the top right-hand corner she had written her name. Not only that, as I began to read through this religious tome, it became apparent that she had written notes in the margins. From what I have read of what others have written about Charlotte, no one else until that point had used this primary piece of evidence in any kind of academic research. Talk about inspirational!

I completed the book by lunchtime and was buzzing with excitement so much that I decided I needed to go for a walk. With a packed lunch in my rucksack I walked out behind the parsonage and across the moor. I have to say I was a little disappointed. I saw no Wuthering Heights that day. It was a beautiful afternoon, with bright sunshine and a cloudless sky, nothing wuthering about it at all. After about four miles, I reached a place called Top Withens, which some have suggested is the location of Wuthering Heights. It is much more likely to be somewhere near to Halifax. This derelict farmhouse wasn't anywhere near big enough, but it was conveniently located on the Pennine Way and within easy walking distance from Haworth for the tourists.

I sat on a dry-stone wall and took out my lunch as a flock of sheep suddenly became incredibly interested in what I was eating. I have never seen sheep so tame. Given half a chance they would have taken my sandwiches right out of my hands. They were clearly accustomed to the number of tourists visiting the area and knew which side their bread was buttered.

Other writers mentioned included John Le Carre, Agatha Christie, Enid Blyton, and Arthur Ransom. One thing we did realise in doing this exercise is that as writers we are all prolific readers. Literature begets more literature, just as creativity gives birth to more creativity. If you want to write, the best advice I can possibly give you is to begin reading. If you haven't read a book in a while, why not go back and read some of the stories that you loved so much when you were a child, like Little Women, The Secret Garden, The Railway Children, Charlie and the Chocolate Factory, or Ballet Shoes. We agreed amongst ourselves that we would all sign up to Goodreads and befriend one another so we could begin recommending our best reads. Even those of us who didn't have as much time to read, or hadn't read a book in a long time, decided to start listening to audio books.

Activity Three: Biographies

As I mentioned when talking about my favourite teacher, I once wrote a biography of Al Capone. This activity involved writing a short biography. It could be someone we knew, a distant ancestor whose stories had been passed down through the generations, or a notable person from history.

Some members of the group wrote about a close family member, many of whom had passed away. Many tears were shed in sharing the writing with the rest of the group, as they found it cathartic to have written that person's story, and the whole process made them feel closer to them.

There were some hilarious stories about more distant relatives, tales of smuggling, debauchery, and even bigamy. A lot of these writers have gone on to start work on a book regaling tales from their family's history.

The third group wrote about notable people from history. One wrote about Elvis Presley. It was amazing how much they knew about his life and they were clearly a fan. Another wrote about Florence Nightingale because they had recently watched a documentary about her life. One wrote about Henry the Eighth because they were taught the rhyme about his wives at school and had memorised their names. Not only this, but they had been an avid reader of books by Philippa Gregory, Allison Weir and the like.

Not everybody wants to write fiction. Writing biographies is a pleasure in itself but it can also help us to connect to lost loved ones and give us the opportunity to get out of our own heads and into the shoes of another for a while. We can identify with some of the things they struggled with, take delight in that which brought them joy, and develop a deeper understanding of the human condition in order to be able to empathise more with others.

If you were to write a biography of a close family member who would it be? Have you ever researched your family tree? What stories about your ancestors have been passed down from generation to generation? Write them down and perhaps you would like to share them with the rest of your family. Have you ever written a biography of a notable person from history? If you could write one, who would you choose?

Activity Four – Setting the Scene

This exercise involved another visual prompt for which I had put together a selection of images from different types of locations. One was a snow-capped mountain scene from Europe, another a sunset scene over the seaside in Devon, a third was a picture of lush green patchwork fields in rolling countryside. The final image was a panoramic view of London and the Thames. I asked the group to select their favourite picture and to write about it. Gather some images together of different types of scenes and have a go at doing this now.

I picked London. This is what I wrote:

> *The Thames, the artery of this ancient city, pumping life into the muddy banks and sooty buildings. Once derelict warehouses and wharfs transformed into plush apartments and tasty restaurants and bars for the bright young things. The Gherkin on the right, a trailblazer in eccentricity and quirkiness, the Shard on the left, a ruthless, cutting, splitting monument to growth. Tower Bridge, a testament to Victorian engineering, adjacent to the Tower with its many tales of woe. This sprawling metropolis of centuries of innovation and experimentation, of majesty and misery, and this hive of cultural splendour and hotbed of diversity. The watermen in Tudor times, nipping back and forth from south to north, carrying cargo and personages, of palaces and parliaments, of policing and petitioning, this city is a map to the history of growth.*

As we shared what we had written we ended up talking about lockdown and how we haven't been able to go to some of the places and see some of the things which brings us joy. We're quite fortunate, in that all of us live with a foot in two camps, between the countryside and the beautiful city of London. However, because of this lockdown we have all been severely restricted in our movements, unable to go to town and see the cultural things that until now have nourished our souls.

Some of us have become accustomed to being at home, almost institutionalised, and have shared with the group that we would be quite content to stay at home forever so long as we could still see some of our immediate family that we have been isolated from these past few weeks and months. But for others it has been excruciating to be stuck at home and not be able to get out and see the world. There has been some consolation that the world has effectively ground to a halt and so even though they are at home, they're not really missing out on anything because everything is closed. But they are unsettled, dissatisfied, restless and desirous of getting back to some semblance of normality.

But there is also fear. Many of us are terrified about going back out into the world. For the most part we trust the places of business who are going to great lengths to keep us and their staff safe by putting arrows and lines on the floor to show us how far apart to stand and in which direction to walk, but we are fearful of the average person who maybe hasn't been directly affected by COVID-19, who doesn't take it seriously, who thinks it's all a bit of a joke and for whom the rules simply don't apply.

I had one such experience yesterday, and it led me to have a panic attack. I had been emboldened because that morning I had gone to take my car in to be serviced. It was long overdue, having needed to be done in February. The dealership was fantastic. The signs were clear, the arrows were obvious, and there were Perspex shields up between me and the service representative. They were friendly but informative and I felt comfortable following their instructions about dropping off keys on a table and picking them up again afterwards. In short, I felt safe.

I felt so good that I made the decision to visit with my dad that day in an open space. This was the first time that I had seen him in over two months and so I was probably feeling quite emotional although I may not have realised how much at the time. It was a wonderful visit and so good to see him and my stepmother. I had missed them both terribly during this lockdown.

By the time I got home I was exhausted, and so were the other members of my family, so I suggested we would get takeaway that night from a local Italian restaurant. Surely all businesses were taking things as seriously as the dealership had done earlier that day. I was confident that I would be okay, and I would feel safe.

At the allotted time, I went down to collect the food. There were no clear signs on the door as to what the process was but there was already a woman waiting outside and two others inside on either side of the room. The woman outside explained to me that we would queue outside and when one person came out another could go in. That seemed reasonable to me, although I did wonder why the restaurant had not made the decision to make things one way as it covers three shop fronts with three doors. It would have been easy for us to go in one and out another.

As we waited, another man joined the queue behind us, with all of us social distancing. Eventually, someone came out and the woman in front of me went inside. When my time came, I went in and found the owner of the establishment was taking the money using contactless payment across a double table. I still felt safe. As I waited for my food, I took a seat to the left making sure that I didn't touch anything with my gloved hands.

We continued to wait for our food, and this was when the problem occurred. A longer queue had started to form outside and a man who was about three people back in that queue decided to come inside to find out when his food would be ready. He effectively jumped the queue and his demeanour was one of entitlement and insensitivity towards others. He was quite aggressive towards the restaurant owner and then he proceeded to sit down at the table where I was sitting with his daughter. By this stage, I was starting to panic. It had been over two months since I had been in such proximity to people outside of my own immediate family and I felt incredibly uncomfortable.

Things got worse. Because this man had queue-jumped, the people who had been in front of him took it upon themselves to come into the restaurant as well and so before we knew it a space that had been designed for two to three people had eight people in it. Social distancing went out the window. I couldn't get to the door without being less than two metres away from another person. My chest tightened, my breathing became rapid, my lip wobbled, and I desperately tried to keep it together.

The daughter became aware of my distress and asked what she could do to help. But there wasn't anything that she could do. Normally when I have a panic attack someone could sit next to me hold my hand or put their arm around my shoulders, but no one could do that here because we had to remain apart from each other. She did however encourage her dad to move to a greater distance which helped, and for which I am grateful.

What followed was the inquisition from everyone in the room wanting to understand why I was upset and what had triggered it. I was so embarrassed, so ashamed, felt so weak. I didn't want to have to explain myself to everybody, to tell them that I had PTSD, that I was prone to panic attacks in exceptionally stressful situations. Instead I simply told them that I wasn't used to being around people and apologised for what had happened. Thankfully the food arrived at that point and the waves of people parted so that I could get out the door and into the fresh air. I dived in my car and sat there sobbing with my shoulders shaking while I let out all the pain.

You might be wondering why I've written all of this in this book. Because I am a firm believer that if we write it out, if we verbalise our fears and our pains and our shame, it enables us to move towards a greater freedom and is the point at which the healing begins. As we go on this Writing for Wellness journey together, how can I expect other people to be vulnerable, to trust me, to be open, if I'm not prepared to do that myself? Take heart, if you are sitting at home right now absolutely terrified about going out for the first time in a long time, what I would say is this, you are not alone, you are not weak, you are not a freak. Equally, whilst there maybe times of intense pain and sorrow, times of panic and fear, this too shall pass, there will be places you will find in which you feel safe as we move slowly towards the new normal that is tomorrow.

Activity Five – Music as Inspiration

We had already used music to write by, but this activity gave the group the opportunity to select their own music. At the end of one week, I gave them some homework to make a playlist of music that they could listen to while they wrote. They would bring this music with them to the next meeting and then when we began this exercise, they would mute their microphones and listen to the music for 10 minutes while we all wrote together.

After we had written, we shared our writing with each other, and we also shared the contents of the playlists. Several people incorporated famous film scores into their playlists, the most popular being Harry Potter and Star Wars. But Rocky, Flashdance, and Schindler's List also featured.

Others included classical music such as Beethoven's Ode To Joy, Dvorak's New World Symphony, and a Mozart Piano Concerto. Only a few included pieces of music that contained lyrics. Some of these where traditional hymns or songs such as Jerusalem, Land of Hope and Glory, and I Vow to Thee My Country. The person with these hymns in their playlist is sad that they will not be able to go to the Proms this year. Others included songs from their childhood like Dancing Queen by ABBA. Ed Sheeran also featured heavily.

Writing to music that we are already familiar with brings a different kind of inspiration than music that we have yet to hear. The former transports us to places in our memories or inspires us in our endeavours, lifts our mood, or in the case of Flashdance makes us want to dance. The latter forces us to pay closer attention to the undulations of tempo and pitch and to allow our imagination to picture what we're hearing. Both are excellent writing prompts to help us in our journey towards Wellness.

Not everybody enjoyed the experience of writing to music. We had the lady that doesn't like music at all and of course for her this was excruciating. She described it as being like someone was trying to stick a series of needles into her brain. But she wasn't the only one. There were other writers who didn't enjoy writing to music, and instead preferred silence or the buzz of everyday noise around them. As I have said before, ideas in these chapters are merely suggestions for you to take or leave as they are useful to you. Fill up your tool belt with what works for you and leave the rest behind.

Activity Six: From Inspiration to Aspiration

There is a plethora of other ways in which we can become inspired to write. These are just some suggestions to get you thinking about it. Now we have spent some time looking at inspiration, I decided to get the group to start thinking about aspiration. In this exercise we will be writing about what we aspire to do, whether it be in our writing, in our everyday lives or in some other area of interest to us. What do you want to achieve in life? What would you like to create? If it could be in any medium, what would your Opus look like? Set the timer for 10 minutes and begin writing now.

Because of some of the other exercises that we had already done as a group, we were ready for this question. We had already begun to think about our hopes and our dreams, we had spent time drawing from our wells of imagination and igniting with enthusiasm from a spark of inspiration. We were now ready to face our aspirations.

A lot of these involved writing, but not exclusively. One lady's goal was to learn to crochet and to make herself a blanket, another was to learn to bake bread. Another still had the desire to transform her garden from an overgrown tangle of weeds into a haven for butterflies and bees where she could sit on a bench listening to a babbling brook, and watch the flowers grow.

But for many, some of their aspirations did involve writing. This was a powerful realisation for them because a great deal of the people in this group had always loved to write but somewhere along the lines in the course of their lives, they had started to doubt this dream and question their own abilities. These were the people who had joined the group and said they had no imagination and yet slowly but surely over the weeks the writing had relaxed and opened, and they transported us to new places and worlds in the most magical of ways. They had grown in confidence over this time and were now ready to publicly share in this safe space the things that they dreamed of creating.

Some are going to write family histories and have already begun to piece the stories together. One lady aspires to become the next Barbara Cartland, writing a series of romance novels. One woman is putting together a collection of her poems and has decided to take the brave step of publishing them. Another still, who is incredibly musical and plays the guitar, even shared a song with us that he had written. We have encouraged him to record it on YouTube and to upload it to Spotify so that we can stream it on there.

This is another key component of this group that has been so powerful. None of us are in competition with each other. We're not trying to get one over on the other, outdo each other, or become jealous or threatened when someone else creates something beautiful. Quite the contrary, one of the reasons this group has been so profoundly important to each of us is because it is full of unconditional love and support, full of encouragement and positivity. There are no tall poppies being choked by the other poppies here. Instead, we all try and help each other shine, and rise to the sky. It is my hope that no matter where you are in the world that you will find a group that is equally safe, equally loving, and equally encouraging and supportive.

Summary

Inspiration is all around us. It can be found in people, places, things and situations and often where we least expect. Inspiration is the lifeblood of our lives, the air that we breathe and the infilling of our spiritual selves. Aspiration is the outflowing of that inspiration as we continue to become a part of that creative story. Inspiration and aspiration, the breathing in and breathing out, are at the core of what it truly means to be alive. We were born to create and be co-creators with God in the world. Like a parent and child building a sandcastle on the beach let us breathe in and breathe out the inspiration and aspiration of our authentic selves as we express what it means to be human and part of something so much bigger than ourselves.

11 THE DARK SIDE

One of the important challenges faced when leading a Writing for Wellness group is to read the room and get a feel for how people are doing. When I'm able to do this, I can then strike a balance between the lighter, more fun exercises, and those that are a little meatier and heavy. This chapter looks at some of the heavier writing prompts that we have worked through together on our Writing for Wellness journey.

I don't always know how an exercise is going to land. Sometimes it's the most innocuous of prompts that generate the most powerful of responses. A classic example of this is when I asked the group to write about ice cream. But there are some obviously more challenging questions that I have tried to intersperse throughout our time together. Below are just a few of those that we have looked at.

Activity One: It's a Nightmare!

For this exercise I got the group to dive into the realm of their dreams, only this time it was their nightmares. I asked them to try to remember a nightmare, or even a recurring nightmare, that they had experienced in their lives and to write about it. Some found it difficult to remember any of the dreams they had dreamed. For these people I suggested that they get creative and imagine what a nightmare might be.

People didn't cry during this exercise, but they did start to feel unsettled. Their writing brought up for them some of their darkest fears and some of their most painful emotions. I didn't force anybody to keep writing if they didn't want to. When we came to the point of sharing our writing with each other it was interesting to see the transformations that took place as a problem shared became a problem halved and the power that some of these dreams had over people dissipated.

When I was about nine, I started to have a recurring dream, and this is what I wrote about:

I was working as a waitress in a restaurant. My boss was a mean man. He made me do lots of things I didn't want to do. One day, my mum came into the restaurant and my boss made me serve her. But I knew that what he wanted me to serve her, even though it looked like an innocent plate of chips, would be dangerous. But he made me do it, even though I didn't want to, and so I served the plate of chips to my mum and they proceeded to explode in her face.

Although at the time the dream was extremely distressing to me, I now look back on the episode of the exploding chips and find it funny. I suppose it has become for me the equivalent of JK Rowling's Boggart in which I've been able to turn something seemingly sinister into something that is hilarious. How about you have a try and write your nightmares down? Now share them with somebody else and see what happens. How could you turn something distressing into something to be laughed at? How can you reduce the power that it has over you?

Activity Two: Phobias

The next activity that we looked at were our phobias and fears. Again, this is quite a difficult exercise for people. It was relatively easy for the group to write about what it was they were afraid of, and where their phobias lay, but they tended to emotionally distance themselves from their writing at this point and simply stated these phobias as fact without digging any deeper into them. They were quite content with keeping them as they were, in a neat box with a label on top, never to be taken out and looked at. That's okay. There's no right or wrong to any of this, we're just on a journey together to see where it takes us. Take what you need and leave the rest behind!

I still have plenty of phobias and fears myself, but there is one that I have been able to overcome, and that is my fear of spiders. Sure, if one makes the mistake of crawling along the ceiling of my bedroom so that it's immediately above my head then it has earned the right to be ejected unceremoniously out the window, but otherwise I'm quite content to coexist with my eight-legged friends.

Don't get me wrong, it wasn't always this way. Even as an adult, there have been countless times I've screamed my head off in the middle of the night because I've seen a spider in my room and have insisted a family member kill it. But one day something happened which totally changed my perspective. I was outside sitting on a bench and a little way off between two bushes a spider was spinning a web. I was far enough away to feel safe and I suppose because it was outside it did not feel so bad. I conceded, spiders were supposed to be outside. I sat watching this spider at her work. The thing that fascinated me the most was that she kept changing her mind. She would create a pattern and then unravel some of it and go off in a different direction. How could an erratic, dangerous, unprincipled creature have the wherewithal to try to find the optimum way to spin a web to catch the maximum number of flies? She had a brain. She wanted to do well. She wanted to get it right. For the first time ever, I could relate to a spider! How can you be afraid of something when you begin to understand it?

I wasn't the only one who talked about overcoming a fear or a phobia. One lady was afraid of heights. She only had to go two steps up a ladder and she began shaking. She decided that she needed to work on overcoming this, and, not being somebody who did things by halves, she committed to doing a skydive for charity. How she overcame that fear I do not know but she did the skydive and raised over £5,000. Going two steps up the ladder is small fry now in comparison to jumping out of a plane thousands of feet in the air.

Activity Three: Greatest Fears

This exercise is slightly different to our nightmares and our phobias. I asked the group to spend some time writing about their greatest fears. This isn't so much about a fear of spiders or heights, or remembering our nightmares, but is rather an opportunity to write about the things that niggle at us and cause us anxiety on a day to day basis. How about you have a go at doing this now?

Without fail every single person in the group wrote about either themselves or those they loved. Some wrote about dying alone, others about losing those that they loved. There were others who wrote about going through the whole of their lives without finding purpose and meaning, without being able to express their authentic selves to the fullest.

As people wrote about their greatest fears, and began to realise that they had a lot in common with each other, I started to see the group bond with each other even more and began to realise that we weren't just a group of individual writers coming together once a week to take part in some exercises, we were becoming a community, a group of friends who would listen to each other, write to each other, support each other, and love each other. I didn't set out with this intention. I'm not sure I even knew why I was starting the group when I did. It was just an idea that popped into my head one day. I knew I simply had to do it. Have you ever had ideas like that? If your intuition gives you an idea, and you feel strongly that you're supposed to do it, especially if it benefits other people, I would go for it.

The thing I love most about this group is being able to hear another person's writing. For the purposes of this book, all you are getting to hear are anecdotes about what other people said and wrote about and large chunks of my own writing. I will be honest, I'm growing tired of the sound of my own voice, and really look forward to hearing from all of you. Do share your writing online if you feel bold enough or contact me privately and let me know how it is going. If there is room, we would love to have you in our writing group or you could think of starting one of your own. It only takes three or four people to get it off the ground and from that point onwards word begins to spread, and people start to come and join you.

Back to our greatest fears. OK, I'll get the ball rolling, this is what I wrote:

> *My greatest fear is that I'm not good enough, that there is something intrinsically bad about me that people will discover and when they do, they will reject me. My greatest fear is that I am repulsive, unlikeable, unlovable. My greatest fear is that I will live this life without ever achieving anything positive or lasting. My greatest fear is that I will die alone without a loved one by my side.*

Okay, that's enough from me. Over to you.

Activity Four: Knowing Me, Knowing You

I did not plan to put this final activity under this chapter. It seemed like an innocent question, but the reaction it produced in a lot of people was strong and so I thought that this is probably the best place for it. The question that I asked the group was, "what do you want people to know about you?" You have a go at answering it now.

As I said, there were strong reactions to this exercise. One lady didn't feel able to go first in sharing and needed a bit of time to compose herself before she read her writing to the group. When she did, she wrote how she felt that everybody already knew everything that she wanted them to know and that she didn't want anybody to know anything that they didn't already know. This lady is an incredibly private person and I don't think we appreciated just how private until she read this to us. It has helped us to be sensitive to her feelings and her desire for privacy.

Another man, who has mental health issues, wrote about his desire to not be defined by them. He had a fear that this was all that people saw in him and that their perception of him was jaded by the knowledge that he struggled with anxiety and depression. The love that the people in the room felt for him as he read was palpable. I think he began to realise that, far from being defined by any illness he might have, he was accepted, loved and cherished unconditionally by others.

What about you? What do you want us to know about you? How did it make you feel as you wrote it out? Feel free to share it using the hash tag #writingforwellness.

Throughout most of my life I have spent an inordinate amount of time trying to achieve a flat calm. I have now reached the stage where I have realised that no matter how hard I try, no matter how much self-will I employ, the storms of life will inevitably rage. The gift that writing has given me, the ability to vocalise my fears, has helped me to recognise the power source that is outside of myself, bigger than myself, to which I can cling in the storm. In addition to this, I have found a community in which we can share our hopes and dreams, joys and fears, knowing that we belong and will never be alone.

In the next chapter, we will be looking at the headlines of our lives.

12 READ ALL ABOUT IT!

At first glance it might seem that we have already covered this subject in other chapters, but I wanted to incorporate into our Writing for Wellness journey the opportunity for the group to explore different genres of writing. Sometimes we would simply make lists, other times or we would explore poetry, occasionally we would delve into the realm of fiction. In this chapter we used the medium of newspaper and magazine articles, of press releases and headlines.

We have already talked about the importance of reading in fuelling our imaginations and sparking inspiration and aspiration inside of us. I always have at least one book on the go, sometimes a devotional, sometimes a biography or piece of non-fiction, and always both a light read and something that is more challenging. Others prefer to read one book at a time. The important thing is that we read, even if it's a magazine or newspaper.

Imagine you want to learn to knit. Where would you begin? Perhaps you might go to a craft shop and purchase the equipment such as a set of needles, some yarn and a pair of scissors. But if you didn't know how to knit, or didn't have very much experience of knitting, would you simply go home and attempt to cast on? I know if I tried to do that, I would end up with more holes than stitches. No, if I wanted to learn to knit, I might buy a book that would teach me how or perhaps go on YouTube and watch someone show me how to do it. I might join a knitting group so that I could sit with other knitters and learn from them. I wouldn't sit at home on my own with no outside resources to show me how.

The same is true of writing. It is a craft just like knitting. If you want to embark upon a writing journey, you may well go to a stationer and purchase a notebook and some pens. If you're anything like me you're likely to come out with a lot more than that besides. But if you go home and simply begin to write without reading anything about the writing process, without experiencing the work that other people have done, you will be limiting yourself, and deny yourself the opportunity to learn and grow. Refining the craft that is writing is a lifelong adventure and every day is a school day.

Activity One: The Press Release

For this exercise I got the group to write a press release for our Writing for Wellness group. I asked them to think about the who, what, where, when, why and how, and to begin to craft a release that would culminate in a quote from them about the group. Put simply, this is how it would work:

> *Who? - A group of people.*
> *What? - Who write*
> *Where - On Zoom*
> *When? - Thursday mornings from 10:30 AM to 12:30 PM*
> *Why? - To go on a journey towards Wellness*
> *How? - By using a variety of different writing prompts which are shared in a safe, loving, and supportive environment*
> *Quote: "This group has been an absolute life saver for me throughout my time in lockdown. To be able to write about my feelings, to realise that others have those same feelings, has been the highlight of my week. I cannot begin to express what it has meant to me," said Olivia McCabe.*

You may not yet have started your own Writing for Wellness group, but you might like to write a press release about one that is yet to begin. In the quote you could talk about what your hopes are for the group, and what you have heard has happened in other groups. Have a go at writing a release now. If this release is for a group that you are starting or have begun to run, perhaps you might like to share this on social media or send it to your local newspaper.

It was my turn to cry during this exercise. I don't think I had appreciated just how profound an effect this group had had on people during the weeks that we were in lockdown. As I sat there listening to the quotes at the end of the releases and hearing people's testimonials about the gift that this group had been to them, I was absolutely blown away. I had no idea. It was a very humbling experience and I'm simply grateful that I listened to my intuition when I did and took the action necessary to create this space in which people could breathe.

Activity Two: Pyjamas

This was another random writing prompt like ice cream, only this time I asked the group to write a headline which included the word pyjamas. You have a go at doing that now. Once they had written their headlines, I got them to write the full article that went with it. How about you have a go?

Pyjamas is an on-trend subject during lockdown. There have been plenty of jokes flying around the Internet about people having two sets of pyjamas each day, one pair they change into at nine in the morning and the other pair they change into at nine at night. Most of the people in the group made some reference to lockdown in their article about pyjamas. One person even wrote about there being a rush on pyjamas with people stockpiling them in the same way that they have stockpiled toilet paper and hand sanitizer. Here is what I wrote:

Stripy Fabric Stolen from Pyjama Factory
Brian the elephant stole stripy pyjama fabric from the Hoofson Pyjama Factory on Trunk St at midnight last night in order to make a set of pyjamas for his family. He carried the rolls off in the basket on the front of his bicycle.
"I don't know how the people of Ivory Island will cope without their pyjamas!" said factory owner Mr Ronald Hoofson. "When the stolen goods were retrieved, they had already been cut up to make pyjamas for elephants and so the fabric is absolutely ruined!"

Activity Three: Obituary

I was tempted to put this exercise under the Dark Side chapter. At first glance, it can certainly seem morbid. A lot of the writing that we had done up until this point focused on things outside of ourselves and another people. This was one opportunity for us to look at ourselves. Some people found this easier to do than others, not because they were thinking about death, but because they were thinking about themselves. They would have been much more comfortable and confident writing an obituary for someone else. But in this exercise, I asked them to write their own obituary. You do that now.

One person took the humour route and devised a somewhat hilarious way for them to leave this mortal coil and proceeded to talk about the funny sides to their personality and the humorous things they got up to in their life. I don't think I have belly laughed like that in a very long time and it's what we all needed. It's funny how our writing has a way of being exactly the right thing at the right time. It's almost as if we're being guided along the way. This person is a natural comic and I have encouraged him to explore this more in his writing.

For a lot of people, when they started to think about the kind of things that might be written about them, they began to realise that their lives had been full and that they had accomplished a lot. They realised that they were proud of their achievements. This exercise took them one step further from what they wanted other people to know about them to how they wanted other people to remember them. It was an extremely powerful time of sharing.

It also gave the group an opportunity to reflect and think about what they wanted to do with their life moving forwards, and the kinds of things that they would like to see in their obituary at the end of their life. In addition to this, we even got onto the subject of how we would like our funerals to be and what kind of music we would like played. One person even said that they would like to give their body to medical research.

Most of us don't talk about death enough. That doesn't mean to say that we should be discussing it all the time. I am a great believer in the mantra, "get busy living rather than get busy dying," that we should be living in the moment and focusing on the positive, but as we know death is as real as taxes. There is no getting away from it. We are surrounded by it, it is an inevitability for us all, and by writing it out, we become less afraid of it.

It also gave people the opportunity to talk about the other obituaries that they have written in their life, the eulogies that they have given at funerals, and to share some of the grief that they have experienced that they may not have expressed before. I never decide what direction we're going in when I give an activity to the group. I always let it go where it may. Often it surprises me.

Summary

Writing is a craft like any other. it takes time to develop. we get better at it when we learn from others by reading what they have written, by getting feedback from them when we share our own writing, and by learning from books on writing. As we go on this Writing for Wellness journey together there are several different mediums that we can use to express ourselves. Sometimes it's as simple as writing a list, we can express ourselves through poetry and prose, we can even explore the realms of our imagination in creative fiction. We can also write articles and press releases. Any of these genres can become useful tools in unlocking our imaginations or accessing our subconscious as we become free to be well.

In our next chapter we will look at the writing prompts that are first and last lines.

13 FIRST AND LAST LINES

In this chapter we will be looking at different first and last lines that we can use as writing prompts to help us explore what is going on inside us.

Activity One: Once Upon a Time...

Perhaps the most famous first and last lines in history are, "Once upon a time," and, "they all lived happily ever after." We used these lines as prompts in order to write our own fairy tales. You try it now.

One woman wrote about a little girl who loved flowers but who lived with a wicked stepmother who wanted to pave over the garden and get rid of every piece of greenery as far as the eye could see. Another wrote about an imaginary knight of the round table, in the vein of the Arthurian legends, with chivalry and courtly love. A third wrote about people living under the sea and the constant battle that they face in trying to clean up all the plastic. It was incredible to see how a simple fairy tale could incorporate such a meaty subject as climate change.

I wrote a story about a cat called Anastasia:

> *Anastasia was a beautiful, white cat with blue eyes and a little button nose. The only problem was that she knew she was beautiful and was rather spoilt by her owner. She thought she ruled the street where she lived and enjoyed the attention of all the male cats whilst being snooty and ignoring the girl cats.*
>
> *But one day, a new cat moved into the street. Her name was Fatima. She was Persian, and her coat was a silvery grey. She was so exotic that all the other cats in the street started to pay her more attention and began to ignore Anastasia. Anastasia became cross and started to complain to her owner. She became so upset she started to eat more and more and go out less and less. She neglected her coat which became matted and dirty so that*

when she did go out, she was ridiculed by the other cats.

But not Fatima. Fatima was kind and gentle and took Anastasia under her wing and befriended her. She groomed her to clean her coat and played with her so that Anastasia started to become lean and fit again. Because Fatima was so popular, with both the girl cats and the boys, and because she had befriended Anastasia, Annie, as Fatima called her, became popular again too, only this time she remembered and was grateful for all the love and attention that she had received. They all lived happily ever after.

What would your fairy tale look like? Where and when would it be set and what would be its theme? Would you write about princes and princesses, actual fairies, or other mythical creatures? Would you write a morality tale like those who addressed issues of climate change and the pollution of our seas? Would you draw from folklore like the tales of King Arthur, or re-write an old fairy tale in the modern age? As you begin with, "Once upon a time," and end with, "and they all lived happily ever after," you can have almost anything in between.

Activity Two: Because of you...

There are an infinite number of first lines that you can use as writing prompts, but some are especially good when writing for Wellness as they help us to dig deep and uncover what's going on in our subconscious and how we are feeling. The first line that I used in this exercise was, "because of you..." I got the group to write these three words on the page and then set the timer for 10 minutes and asked them to start writing. You do the same now. Here is what I wrote:

Because of you I'm still single. Because of you I'm all alone. Because of you I'm frightened of intimacy. Because of you I may never know the shiver down my spine that comes with holding the hand of someone I love as I walk down the street. Because of you I feel violated, because of you I am afraid, because of you my life will never be the same again. Because of you the choice was taken away from me. Because of you I'm damaged goods. Because of you the innocence has left me and what is left behind is a sordid pile of meat.

That's what I used to think. I don't think that now. You do not have the final say. You may have taken it away from me, you may have caused me pain and shame and self-disgust. But you do not have the last word. I am beautiful, I was made that way and nothing that anybody can do will take that away from me. I am beautiful inside and out and I have a heart that longs to beat alongside that of another, that longs to fall into step with another soul. I have a hand that will one day hold the hand of another, a spine that will shiver, a story that will be told. But you don't feature in it, because you don't count, you are nothing to me but a throw away comment in a footnote on a long-forgotten page. I will arise and survive. I will arise and be born anew. I am pure and clean and fresh and innocent. There is always hope for a brighter tomorrow. There is nothing that has been made that cannot be made new.

Okay, so I went a little deeper with that then I had perhaps intended, but I wasn't the only one. Most people treated it as a gratitude list, acknowledging the things that someone had done for them that had been positive in their lives. They acknowledged the ways in which the inspiration, encouragement and support of others had enabled them to do things that they might not have been able to do otherwise. But some took this exercise as an opportunity to vent, to process their frustrations and anger towards another in a safe environment. There's nothing shameful about doing this and that's why I have shared quite a personal story with you here and have been quite open in other places in this book. It's not to elicit sympathy, or to ask you to fix me. I don't need that right now. It's simply to demonstrate that it's better out than in, and it's by writing it out that we can go on a journey that will hopefully lead us out of the valleys and onto the mountaintops where we can see a brighter future ahead.

Activity Three: The Last Word

This exercise was more about the last paragraph or chapter of a book it was about the actual last word. We spend a little bit of time talking about famous last words and the openings to famous last chapters. A classic example of this is the beginning of the last chapter in Jane Eyre in which for the first time she directly addresses the reader and writes the immortal line, "Reader, I married him." When you know the context in which those words were written they carry such a powerfully emotional punch in which we join with Jane in our jubilation that she has finally found a way to unite with her soul mate om equal terms.

If you were to write the last line of a story about a woman or man in search of their soul mate, how would you begin the last chapter, or what would be the last line? Spend some time writing about that now. Many of the group who worked on this exercise ended up going off on tangents talking about what it meant to have a soul mate, whether or not they had found a soul mate in their life, whether they were still with that soul mate, and, if they were still searching for that soul mate, what that soul mate looked like to them. You just never know where the pen will take you! Go with the flow!

Activity Four: The 5/5/5 Challenge

Thankfully, all the members of the group are prolific readers and are Luddites enough to still have bookshelves, otherwise this exercise wouldn't have worked quite so effectively. I asked them to go to their bookshelf, or in some cases their fifth bookshelf, and to take down the fifth book from the top and bring it back to where we were working. I then asked them to turn to the fifth page in the book and then to look for the fifth sentence on that page. That sentence then became their writing prompt and we set the timer for 10 minutes and began to write. You do that now. If you don't have any physical books in the house and you prefer to use an E-reader, that's fine. Just pick the fifth book in your electronic library and do the same thing.

My book was, "A Woman Unknown," by Lucia Graves. My sentence was, "only the white two-story house that had been my home seemed unchanged as I drove past it in the early evening." Here is what I wrote next:

Even the geraniums were blooming from the hanging baskets and the terracotta pots that surrounded the front door. A cat had stretched on the white wall to the back garden, and I longed to climb the trellis as I'd done as a teen and look inside. As the image flashed past me, I took a mental snapshot of it and wondered who was living there now. Is there a girl like me who picks the ripe oranges to be squeezed every morning and who chews the figs directly from the trees? Does she go down to the very end of the garden when frustrated and angry so she can grit her teeth and clench her fists, have a good stomp and scream? What kind of a family were living there now?

I wound my way up the mountainside in my little car that struggled with the steepness of the road. I shifted gear to give it a little more oomph and pulled into the driveway of the country hotel where I was staying. A man in a uniform, hurriedly putting on his hat, emerged from around the corner and took my keys while I climbed the marble steps and went inside. I was blasted with the cool air of the foyer and shivered, pulling my cardigan closer around my shoulders.

"Well?" said Jack, folding his paper and standing when he saw me. "What did you find out?"

"It's still there," I said as we walked into the restaurant and out on to the patio for some lunch. "It hasn't changed much."

"Is that a good or a bad thing?" he asked as he pulled back my chair for me to sit down.

I rocked my head from side to side as I thought about his question.

"Good, I suppose," I said, lifting my sunglasses on to my head and picking up the menu. "But I don't think I want to see it again."

"Why's that?" asked Jack as the sommelier came over and Jack ordered some wine.

"Because I've changed. I'm not the same girl I was when we lived there. I've moved on."

Jack smiled and took my hand, rubbing the large diamond on my finger.

"Good," he said. "It sounds like you're ready to go home."

"You bet I am," I said as I pictured our brownstone home in New York City, the scent of the deli on the corner, and the walks in Central Park. "Yes, Jack, let's go home."

Whilst my contribution ended up being a work of pure fiction, for others the selection of the book itself brought with it some powerful memories and emotions. One lady selected a book that reminded her of her childhood in Africa, another picked a book that had an inscription from her mother inside the flyleaf. Others wrote about themselves from their prompt, or someone they loved. It is always so interesting to see how differently people interpret these prompts, and I suspect that if we were to repeat them over and over, we would illicit a different response every time. I know that is certainly the case with me.

Summary

First and last lines, used in a variety of different ways, are an excellent way to prompt us to write. The beauty of writing this way is that you never know what is going to come from it, and no two interpretations are the same. Even the same person, using the same prompt, will write something different every time. Some of these prompts inspire us to write creative fiction, others to look more at our own lives or those of someone we know. The more ways in which we look to unlock the realm of the imagination, and allow ourselves to come to a safe space and time in which to share our memories, the more we will be able to process sometimes complex emotions and find a new freedom in our lives. How about you devise a list of first lines to use as writing prompts for yourself and dip into them occasionally. Do share them with others using the hash tag #writingprompts and if you want to share them with me, use #writingforwellness as well.

In the next chapter, we will spend some time looking at how the remaining sense of smell, taste and touch can prompt us in our writing, and how some sense can evoke more powerful emotions than others.

14 IT ALL MAKES SENSE

We've already spent quite a bit of time looking at visual and audible prompts for writing. In this chapter we're going to look at the remaining senses of smell, taste and touch. All the senses have the capacity to trigger memories, spark the imagination, and help us get in touch with our feelings. Some of these activities took a little bit of preparation and homework, but what we discovered as a result made all the effort worthwhile.

Activity One: Aromatherapy

For this exercise, I sent the group a small gift package each. In it was a bottle of almond oil along with a selection of aromatherapy essential oils. As we met as a group, I asked them all to select one scent and to add a couple of drops of it to a palm of olive oil. They then rubbed this into their wrists. I then set the timer for ten minutes and asked them to write about whatever came into their mind as they sat there smelling this scent. This is an opportunity for you to explore the world of smell. How about you buy your own aromatherapy kit with a selection of oils and try for yourself. Be careful not to apply any essential oil directly on the skin as it burns. Always add it to the almond oil first.

One lady selected lavender. It reminded her of her grandmother's wardrobe, and the scent of her handkerchiefs. As she wrote she talked about going to visit her grandmother as a child down in Somerset, the purple swirly carpet in the hallway and the silver brush set on the dresser in the bedroom.

As she continued to write however, and the effects of the lavender caused her to relax, she began to write about her body relaxing, and drifting off into an afternoon nap on a lazy summer's day in the garden. She wrote about closing her eyes and hearing the buzz of the bees and the splash of water as children played in the paddling pool next door. The scene triggered her imagination and caused her to close her eyes in her head. Instead of the imagination triggering images, it triggered sounds.

Another lady selected bergamot. This is my favourite scent too and one that I find particularly useful when I want to be creative. Just rubbing a little bit of this in the almond oil onto my wrists seems to give my brain permission to think outside the box. This was certainly true for the lady who selected it. She wrote about a fantastic world, where everything was iridescent, pearly white. It was a kingdom that was ruled by the Pearl Queen.

Another writer chose lemongrass because he said it made him feel more awake. He didn't want to put the pen down at the end of his writing. He kept saying, "just one more sentence, nearly there!" He wrote about fast moving action, with helicopter gunships flying low over the beaches of the Isle of Wight. Perhaps this will be a big blockbuster film one day.

For some, the oils triggered memories, for some it sparked their imaginations, and for others it made them feel quite emotional. One writer shared that their scent made them feel angry, rambunctious and belligerent. It was certainly an interesting exercise and the group all agreed that they would like to try to do something like this again in the future. Many of them wanted to read about aromatherapy in greater detail and explore the use of the scents in their everyday lives and Writing for Wellness journey.

Activity Two: Perfumes

In a similar vein, for this activity, I asked the group to find some perfume, aftershave or other scented item such as a candle or even soap, and to bring it to the group with them. We then set the timer for ten minutes as usual and began writing. This was a powerful one for some people. One lady had a bottle of her mother's perfume and the tears flowed as she sniffed at it and wrote about the different memories that she had of her mother wearing it.

Another talked about the aftershave they had and wrote about the first date they had gone on with their future wife and how they had been a little liberal with the application of the aftershave. Another wrote about the bar of soap that they had in their downstairs toilet. It was Pears soap which had been used in the family for generations going back as far as they could remember. It hadn't even crossed their mind until this point that smells could be just as much an important part of painting the picture of family history as any other sense could be.

I wrote about one perfume that I have in my collection and that is Venezia by Laura Biagiotti. This is what I wrote:

I was 17 and had to drop out of school. This wasn't because I was academically struggling or because I had a problem with my behaviour, but rather because I was still getting over glandular fever and couldn't keep up with the work because of the number of days I was off sick. I just decided to take the rest of the year off to fully recover and would then go and take my A-levels in Six-form college the following year.

Towards the end of that year of recovery, I was strong enough to do some temporary work and landed myself quite a lucrative office job. Still living at home, and not paying rent, this left me with a sizeable amount of disposable income, especially for a 17-year-old.

One day, I was flicking through the pages a Vogue magazine when I came to an advert for a perfume. It was Venezia by Laura Biagiotti. By opening the folds on the edge of the page I could smell the scent. It was fruity and aromatic, sweet but woody, and I was absolutely captivated by it. I don't think I have been quite so enchanted by a perfume either before or since. I was determined to get my hands on a bottle.

It said in the advert that it was only available in Harvey Nichols in London. I made plans to go to Knightsbridge. That day was an adventure. I ate afternoon tea in Simpsons on the Strand, I bought my first Ted Baker shirt which was made of a cranberry silk with a little hood on the back, and I bought a bottle of Venezia by Laura Biagiotti. I sat there sniffing it on the train all the way home while the other passengers just stared.

That wasn't the only bottle I bought. I didn't wear it every day and I made it last, but over the years, despite having other perfumes, this remained my firm favourite. But then the unthinkable happened. It became discontinued. I thought my life was over, not literally of course, but I was bitterly disappointed.

I eked out the remaining dredges of the bottle in my possession and then, with the advent of eBay I started to look for other bottles online, but by this stage my disposable income had severely shrunk and I couldn't afford the hundreds of pounds that people were charging.

But they brought it back and it's for sale again or was until I just checked and cannot find it again!!! I've e-mailed them so fingers crossed! I was so excited when I found this out. OK, I had to order it directly from Italy, but it was worth every penny and still brings me much joy. It just seems to sit so well on my skin and makes me feel sexy and alive again.

If you were to bring the perfume, aftershave, candle, soap or other scented item to a Writing for Wellness group, what would it be? How would it smell and how would you describe it? What would you write? Set your timer for 10 minutes and begin to write now.

Activity Three: Coffee

This activity was yet another simple writing prompt. I got the group to write the word coffee at the top of the page, we set the timer for ten minutes, and began to write. Just as with ice cream, our writing took us down varied paths and unlocked surprising memories and emotions from within.

A lot of people wrote about the hustle and bustle of meeting friends and family in coffee shops. For many, before lockdown, this had been a regular feature of their week. It would have been unthinkable before lockdown that this lifestyle would ever have ground to a halt so abruptly, and now we are faced with going back out into the world, many wrote about how this is likely to change for them moving forwards. Whilst they may consider buying a takeaway coffee and sitting in a park to drink it, they are much more likely to invite somebody around to their house for coffee than they are to meet them in a public place.

Life in many respects will go back to the way it was during my childhood. Back then, we only ate out on special occasions like birthdays. We only bought drinks and other food items when we were on holiday or on a day out, such as ice creams on the beach, or a cup of tea at a National Trust property.

In recent years, I have started to eat out more and more, to the extent where I had begun to eat out more than I had eaten in. Since lockdown, that has obviously changed. The net result is I have eaten less and saved an enormous amount of money. It is my desire, as we emerge from lockdown, to entertain at home more, to have friends around for coffee and to host small dinner parties.

Some members of the group wrote about their anxieties about getting food delivered every week, about staying up until midnight to grab the newly released delivery slots from the various supermarkets online. Some talked about the monotony of their day and as with T.S. Elliot, in his poem, *The Lovesong of J Alfred Prufrock*, they have begun measuring out their days with coffee spoons.

This prompt was a useful exercise in getting people to think about their lives before during and after lockdown and how they feel about it all. You do that now. Write the word coffee at the top of the page, set your timer for ten minutes and just begin to write. Don't worry about where the writing takes you. There is no right or wrong to your writing. Let the words flow.

Activity Four: The Taste Test

This was the exercise that involved the most amount of preparation. I asked the group to bring samples of five different types of taste: something salty, something sweet, something sour, something bitter, and something savoury or umami.

We worked our way through the tastes in turn just putting a little bit of it on our tongues and then writing. A lot of people couldn't taste the bitter, but everything else triggered some really interesting pieces of writing, from memories of trips to the sweet shop on a Saturday morning to spend their pocket money on penny and half penny sweets, to the fish and chips on a Friday night hanging out with friends as a teenager, to the first time they tasted homemade lemonade and had sucked on a lemon thinking it would be as sweet as an orange.

This exercise conjured up some amazing memories, but it also triggered some beautifully descriptive writing. One woman has this uncanny ability to paint pictures with words and to transport us into the heart of the action so that we feel that we are there. This writer was one of the people who at the beginning of our journey together didn't think they had much of an imagination, but they have since given themselves permission to think outside the box and it has unlocked something in them so they are daring to dream and write. They are one of the people who have now joined our writers' group on a Tuesday afternoon where we sit together and write whatever it is that we are working on. I'm really looking forward to reading more of what she and the others have written.

Activity Five: A Touch Of...

A journey through the senses wouldn't be complete without touch. For this exercise I got the group to look around their house and find something soft, something hard, something rough and something smooth. They brought these items back to their desks and we began to write about them in turn using descriptive language for how they felt rather than what they looked like. Many of the writers spent a bit of time with their eyes closed just holding the objects in their hands before they began to write.

This writing prompt, as with some of the others, surprised us in many ways. Someone bought a cushion for their soft object and proceeded to write about a time when they were sick as a child and the sheets on their bed were changed. She rested her head against the fresh, soft pillow. Another writer brought a large key as their hard object. It unlocked the door of the local church for which they were a key holder. They ended up writing about the day that Princess Diana died. The atmosphere in the United Kingdom during that time was one of intense mourning, and he had received a number of calls that day from people who do not normally go to church to ask if the church could be opened so that people could go inside and sit and reflect. He said in his writing that this was the single most important occasion when he had unlocked the church doors because it welcomed people in who had never been before and gave them a safe space in which to grieve and meditate. When he came back to the church later in the evening to lock up again, he found a single white rose on the altar.

You have a go at this exercise now. Find something hard, something soft, something rough, something smooth and take it in turns to hold those objects in your hands while you keep your eyes closed and then write. Don't forget to share your work using the hash tag #writingforwellness.

Summary

In this chapter we spent some time using the senses of smell, taste and touch as writing prompts. We explored aromatherapy, used perfumes as triggers for memories, and took the writing prompt, 'coffee,' letting the words flow. We did the taste test and saw where that took us in our writing and ended by exploring the world of touch.

Whenever we do a different prompt it affects people in a variety of ways. For some, it brings out humour, and for others beautiful descriptions. There were those for whom it brought up memories, both painful and joyful. What all these exercises did, to varying degrees and in different ways, was gave us a safe space in which to explore our feelings about ourselves, others and the world around us. We increased in our self-awareness, gave ourselves space to vent and to grieve, and gave ourselves permission to think outside the box and to dream up the kind of world that we would like to live in.

In our next chapter we will look at what it means to be in search of self. Who are we? Why are we here? What brings us joy, and what is our purpose and meaning in this world? Join us as we continue this journey together.

15 IN SEARCH OF SELF

One of the things I am most passionate about in life is equipping and empowering people to use the gifts and skills that they have been given in order to thrive. It has been an absolute privilege to be able to do something of that within this group and on this journey. Hesitant, shy writers, who had joined this group not even certain why they were there, have grown in confidence over the weeks and really come into their own. Nothing brings me more joy than seeing another person come alive. But that's who I am, what about you? In this chapter we will explore some writing prompts that help us to begin to think about what brings us joy, where our gifts and skills may lie, and how we can express ourselves to the fullest in our lives.

Activity One: The Style Test

This was another visual prompt that I had a lot of fun putting together. I made a collage of images of people with different styles of dress. It could easily have been a collage of the Spice Girls. One image was that of a classic dresser, another wearing sportswear, another casual clothing, another vintage, and another more punk-like in appearance. I asked the group to select the image that they felt represented them the best and then to write about it.

One woman, the philosopher in the group, has been talking about shaving her head since the beginning of lockdown. She hasn't had the necessary equipment at home to do this, so she still has a full head of hair, but I wouldn't put it past her. She selected the vintage dresser and not the punk. This was interesting, if not surprising. She is true to her style in that she loves to wear vintage clothes, and this is something that we have always known about her and have enjoyed. But there is a little bit of her personality that I suspect would like to be punk. I wonder if a new style will begin to emerge that we could call punk vintage or vintage punk.

One woman found this exercise difficult. She has massive issues with her body image and found it painful to focus on the clothes that she would wear. She prefers to wear loose-fitting, baggy clothes but there is a part of her inside that would like to dress differently if only she had the courage to do so. As she wrote, it did trigger her to tears as she talked about the pain that had been caused by people over the years mocking her and bullying her at school for her shape and size, but the more she wrote the further through this dark tunnel she went, and began to emerge into the light on the other side. She arrived in the land where people celebrate the wondrous variety of different shapes and sizes that are our bodies. This was a land in which she was nurtured and appreciated and loved and, in that land, she wore pretty dresses that fit neatly on her body and made her want to twirl and dance.

How about you have a go at selecting some images of people wearing different styles of clothing and in your group get everybody to pick one of those styles that most closely represents them. Then write about it and see where the writing takes you. The important thing is that there is no right and wrong to any of this, there is only the journey, and the beautiful thing about doing this in a group is that you are not alone, people are walking alongside you, loving you every step of the way into Wellness.

Activity Two: On the Other Hand

I'd never done this activity before with a group and so it was interesting to see what would happen. I explained to everyone that we were going to be writing a dialogue between our adult and childhood selves but that when we spoke as an adult we would write with our dominant hands, and when we wrote as a child we would write with our opposite hands. One lady immediately piped up with the fact that she was ambidextrous, but I still challenged her to think about the hand she wrote with the most being her adult hand and the other hand being that of her childhood self.

The dialogues that came out of this exercise were incredibly powerful and probably more so because the child's handwriting looked like that of a child. It enables people to tap into that child inside of them and then as an adult speak to them in a loving and nurturing way. All the fears and concerns that child had could be addressed by an adult that knew exactly what to say. It was powerful and beautiful to see and hear.

One person wrote about the fears they had as they hid in their bedroom while their parents were arguing downstairs. The child in them felt responsible for what was happening, and their adult self was able to reassure them that they were not alone and that it was not their fault.

I wrote about the time that I thought it would be a really good idea to try and cut my own fringe with a pair of my mother's dress making scissors. I must have been about four And I can still remember standing precariously on my bed as the mattress caused me to rock from side to side as I stood looking in the mirror that was above my bed. What resulted was a palpable step in my fringe between the left and the right-hand side.

It was bad enough that it was a school day, but what made matters worse, to my undying shame and embarrassment, was that it was also the day of the school photograph, so my one and only attempt at hairdressing has been immortalised in photographic print. I found that my younger self was embarrassed and felt bad for getting into trouble, but I also discovered that my younger self had a humorous and playful side that could at least see how funny it was. The older and the younger me giggled together as we talked it through.

How about you try this exercise in your group now. What did you discover?

Activity Three: Pen Names

This activity was short and sweet, or so we thought. I simply asked the group to imagine what their pen name or stage name would be. But then one member reminded us of that thing that goes around occasionally of knowing what your porn name would be with your first name being the name of your first pet and your last name being your mother's maiden name or the street where you grew up. Mine would be Jupiter Warren. We fell into hysterics as we shared our names with each other, and we never did get down to writing what our pen names would be.

It is so important when leading a group like this to go with the flow and see where it takes us. I was belly laughing so hard and I know that I wasn't the only one. The tears were flowing down our cheeks but for all the right reasons. This was a good cry, a good laugh and precisely what we needed at the time. If you are having a go at leading such a group, read the room and go with the flow.

Activity Four: A Walk in The Woods

This activity is a commonly used psychological test which helps us examine our relationships. We used a version of it while we were at school. I'm going to ask you a series of questions and as I do, I want you to simply write down the answer. Don't think too much about it, always go with your first instinct, and let's see where this journey takes us. Let us begin.

Imagine that you are in a wood. Who are you walking with?

As you continue your walk through the woods you come across an animal. What kind of animal is it? You approach the animal. What does the animal do?

You're walking further and further into the woods and you come upon a clearing. There's a house in the middle of the clearing. How big is the house? Is it fenced in or not?

As you walk up to the door of this house you see that it is open. You go inside and see a table. Write what you see on and around that table.

As you leave by the back door, you find a cup on the ground. What is the cup made of? What do you do with the cup?

As you walk to the edge of the clearing you find yourself at a body of water. What kind of body of water is it? You must cross this body of water in order to get home. How wet do you get crossing the water?

Before I come to the explanation of these answers, I'll share what I wrote:

I was walking with my mum through the woods. The animal that I came across was a rabbit and when I approached gently crouching down and holding out my hand, it came towards me and started sniffing at my fingers looking for food. As I walked further and further into the woods and came upon a clearing the house that I saw was a large wooden log cabin with smoke rising from the chimney. It was not fenced in. When I went into the house and came across the table, I noticed that there were bowls of fresh fruit on it and bowls of steaming hot soup. Around the table was a family, a husband a wife and three children were sitting at wooden stools and eating their soup while they tore off hunks of crusty bread and slices of cheese.

As I left through the back door, I noticed a porcelain cup on the ground. It was beautifully decorated with silver and blue and I couldn't understand why it was there, so I attached it to the back of my rucksack and kept on walking. The body of water that I found myself in front of was a wide river with large rocks causing rapids and spray. The noise was deafening, but I found a way to cross it so that only the soles of my walking boots got wet.

That was me, what about you? When the group did this, we had a variety of answers and some of them were extremely revealing and provided food for thought. They really enjoyed this exercise as it was a fun way to explore what was going on inside of them.

Now for the great reveal. The person that you are walking with is the most important person in your life. I wasn't at all surprised to discover that this was my mum. I am definitely very close to her. That doesn't mean to say I'm not close to other members of my family. Given the chance, I would probably have had a whole walking group with me. But just for that day that's who I chose to spend my time with.

One lady chose to walk alone. She's not lonely, and she loves people, but what I think this probably told her about herself was that she's incredibly comfortable in her own company and amazingly self-assured.

The size of the animal that you come across on your path represents the size of the problems in your life. I was very happy to hear about this particularly because I'd picked quite a small animal. If the action is more severe it means that you tend to be more aggressive and if the action is more peaceful then you tend to be more peaceful. I am at the peaceful or passive end of the spectrum, but I'm not afraid to stand up for my truths when I need to. What about you what you? What animal did you see and how did you react?

The size of the home that you see is representative of the size of your ambition. Mine is reasonably large but not excessive. One person described an enormous mansion the size of Blenheim or Chatsworth. I spent some time with him after our meeting discussing what his ambitions were and how he might start putting them into action.

If there wasn't a fence around the home, it means that you tend to be more open and this is the case for me as you will have found in reading this book. I am not a private or secretive person at all, although I am hugely sensitive and appreciative of the desire for privacy in others. I just am a great believer that the truth sets you free and that it's always better out than in.

If what you saw on the table wasn't either food, people sitting round it or flowers then this indicates some unhappiness in your life. What a relief that I not only had food and plenty of it but also people as well. Now why didn't I think of flowers? I love having flowers in the house. When some people realised that this was an indication of their level of happiness they wanted to talk about it and I suggested that they go away and journal about what it is that is causing them unhappiness and then at the beginning of the next session they had the opportunity to share their findings with the group if they were comfortable with doing so.

The durability of the cup represents how strong your relationship is with the person in the first part of the story. This was interesting for me because there was a fragility to that cup even though it was intact, but there was also a lot of love, care and attention put into it. It was a thing of beauty and quality. I suppose if I'm going to completely psychoanalyse my response, I would say that I have a good relationship with my mum but that it is something that is precious that needs to be looked after and invested in.

Now this is where things started to get funny and interesting. The size of the body of water is related to the size of your sexual drive. I think the less said about that the better. There are only so many things that I'm really open about. Interestingly enough of course my feet didn't get very wet, so if you're going to take this interpretation literally, I would appear to be a heap of contradictions. One to ponder.

How did you do? The important thing to remember is that this is a bit of fun. It is not an exact science, but rather an opportunity to be creative and explore things in a different way.

Summary

In this chapter we introduced some writing prompts that gave us the opportunity to start looking at who we are, what our place is in this world and what our gifts and skills might be. It gave us the chance to reflect on how we feel about ourselves and others, whether we are passive or aggressive (or both), whether we are happy or frustrated, and even what our sense of style might be.

We are coming close to the end of our journey together and in the final chapter we will ask ourselves the question, where do we go from here?

16 WHERE DO WE GO FROM HERE?

When we began our Writing for Wellness journey a little over ten weeks ago, we had no idea where that journey would take us. For some of us, we didn't even know why we were there, perhaps joining the group because we had nothing else to do whilst in lockdown. This was an opportunity to spend some time with other people we knew online. For others, we have always had a love of writing, whether it be journalling, poetry or prose, and jumped at the opportunity to be able to be together with other writers and share our work.

In the beginning, we lacked any self-belief, thought we weren't very good at writing, that we lacked imagination. We thought we were already well and didn't really need to be on a Writing for Wellness journey at all. We were reticent, nervous, and afraid to think outside the box and dream.

As the weeks went by, we started to trust the group and appreciate the safe, loving space in which we found ourselves once a week. We started to be open with each other through our writing, to explore the realm of the imagination, to dig deep into our memories, and to fearlessly and unapologetically express our emotions. We allowed our imaginations to blossom and, corner by corner, over time we began weeding the garden of our souls, pruning back the overgrown bushes and allowing the flowers to bloom and the fruit to ripen.

We experienced joy, sorrow, laughter and tears, and everything else in between on this journey. We have loved it so much that we haven't wanted it to end, so we have decided that even when lockdown is over, we're going to continue to meet once a week via Zoom in order for everybody to be able to continue to participate in the group no matter where they live.

This group has not only been a support for us during our time of lockdown, a safe space for us to share with each other, a loving and nurturing environment in which we can explore what it truly means to be alive and well, it has also been a hot bed for budding writers. A separate Zoom group for those who want to work towards publication has come out of this Writing for Wellness group. Who knows where it will lead?

I hope that this book has given you some ideas about what it means to explore the realm of the imagination, dig deep into your memory bank, and to find a safe place in which to write it out and release your feelings. I also hope that this book has inspired you in some way to start a group of your own and it is my sincere belief that if you do, and if you uphold the principles of love, support and acceptance of each other, that this will become a safe space for you too. I would love to hear about your group.

My greatest desire is that each of you would know that you are beautiful inside and out, you have something unique and special to give to the world, there is purpose and meaning to your life, and you are loved. It is my hope that, as you start to embark upon your Writing for Wellness journey, you will find that love, support and acceptance, and that you will rise up, like a phoenix from the flames, and embrace the fullness of what it means to be human, co-creators with God, of what it means to be alive.

As I have shared the writing of this book with the members of my group, a few of them have asked if they could send me a short word on what the group has meant to them. I would much rather you hear from them than from me, so here is what they have had to say:

> *"Thank you so much for running the writing for wellness classes. I have enjoyed so much the realisation that I can write and express my thoughts in writing that other people can enjoy. It has certainly been the highlight of my week. Thank you once again."* Mazza

> *"This group would be the highlight of any week but during Lockdown it has been a lifeline as well. One of the best, if not the best, group I have ever been a part of. The bonds that we have formed are indestructible."* Anna

> *"When Olivia told me the name of the group is 'Writing for Wellness' - I did wonder if it was going to be the group for me as I have not been unwell either physically or mentally. WELL - how wrong I was to worry about the title of the group because not only is it the perfect name for many reasons - it is a life changer in every way! However, Olivia is the important factor - she has a very special way of bringing out just the right thing at the right time in all of us. I have called her (hope she doesn't mind) and think of her as an 'emotional guide dog' because she is guiding us all with great skill and gentleness along this new path."* Felicity

> *"I didn't know what to expect when I joined this group nearly ten weeks ago. What I found was and is a supportive environment ably led by Olivia. Through the medium of writing, I could begin to express my thoughts. By using a variety of techniques from single word, story starters,*

free writing, and guided tasks, I have begun to unlock the inner creative ME. I have never felt judged, only valued for what I as an individual bring to the group. If anyone struggles, support is instant. As a group we have laughed and cried together and separately, shared past life events and looked forward to the future. Writing for Wellness has become the highlight of my week —- thank you Olivia and all the members of the group." Sue

"I really felt included, even across zoom the group exuded a warmth that I have not felt in a while. Obviously, I do not want lockdown to last forever, but I hope this group will." Frimette

ABOUT THE AUTHOR

Olivia McCabe is an author, blogger and podcaster from Hertfordshire, England. With a background in publishing, public relations and pastoral care, she has decades of experience working with people as they write their way to Wellness.

A keen crafter, writer and avid reader, Olivia McCabe is passionate about exploring the source of our inspiration and imagination and equipping and empowering people to share their gifts and talents with the world.

You can find out more from Olivia McCabe at www.oliviamccabe.com.

Printed in Poland
by Amazon Fulfillment
Poland Sp. z o.o., Wrocław

61763424R00060